The Two Horizons Old Testament Commentary

J. Gordon McConville and Craig Bartholomew, *General Editors*

Two features distinguish The Two Horizons Old Testament Commentary series: theological exegesis and theological reflection.

Exegesis since the Reformation era and especially in the past two hundred years emphasized careful attention to philology, grammar, syntax, and concerns of a historical nature. More recently, commentary has expanded to include social-scientific, political, or canonical questions and more.

Without slighting the significance of those sorts of questions, scholars in The Two Horizons Old Testament Commentary locate their primary interests on theological readings of texts, past and present. The result is a paragraph-by-paragraph engagement with the text that is deliberately theological in focus.

Theological reflection in The Two Horizons Old Testament Commentary takes many forms, including locating each Old Testament book in relation to the whole of Scripture — asking what the biblical book contributes to biblical theology — and in conversation with constructive theology of today. How commentators engage in the work of theological reflection will differ from book to book, depending on their particular theological tradition and how they perceive the work of biblical theology and theological hermeneutics. This heterogeneity derives as well from the relative infancy of the project of theological interpretation of Scripture in modern times and from the challenge of grappling with a book's message in Greco-Roman antiquity, in the canon of Scripture and history of interpretation, and for life in the admittedly diverse Western world at the beginning of the twenty-first century.

The Two Horizons Old Testament Commentary is written primarily for students, pastors, and other Christian leaders seeking to engage in theological interpretation of Scripture.

Ruth

James McKeown

WILLIAM B. EERDMANS PUBLISHING COMPANY
GRAND RAPIDS, MICHIGAN / CAMBRIDGE, U.K.

Published 2015 by

Wm. B. Eerdmans Publishing Co.

2140 Oak Industrial Drive N.E., Grand Rapids, Michigan 49505 /

P.O. Box 163, Cambridge CB3 9PU U.K.

www.eerdmans.com

Printed in the United States of America

21 20 198 18 17 16 15   7 6 5 4 3 2 1

Library of Congress Cataloging-in-Publication Data

McKeown, James.

   Ruth / James McKeown.

     pages   cm.   — (The Two Horizons Old Testament Commentary)

     Includes bibliographical references.

     ISBN 978-0-8028-6385-0 (pbk.: alk. paper)

     1. Bible. Ruth — Commentaries.   I. Title.

     BS1315.53.M39   2015

     222'.3507 — dc23

                                2014027620

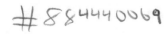

Contents

Acknowledgments

Writing a book is sometimes considered a lonely task. This has not been my experience. I have been greatly encouraged by the help received from many people who have allowed me to discuss the work with them. Top of the list is the editor Gordon McConville and the staff at Eerdmans Publishing Company. Also staff and students at both Belfast Bible College and Union Theological College, where I lectured on Ruth, have been most helpful. In particular I think most appreciatively of the late Mrs. Liz Reid, who attended many of my lectures and helped with insightful questions and comments. We miss her greatly and I know that she would have been one of the first to read this book. I have also benefited from membership of the Society for Old Testament Study. It is a great privilege to attend conferences where distinguished scholars are only too delighted to share their expertise. My thanks are due to them all, but they are not to blame for the particular focus of the book; that responsibility rests with me alone.

Although I mention my family last, this is not an indication of lack of importance. Audrey, my wife, has been a pillar of strength and encouragement, and she fully deserves the same accolade that Boaz gave Ruth when he referred to her as a "worthy woman." I also take this opportunity to dedicate this book to my mother, Mary, and my late father, Wilson.

Preface

I accepted the opportunity to write a commentary on Ruth immediately after completing a commentary on Genesis. At that time this choice was based on the availability of this project. However, as I began work on Ruth, I became aware that this was an excellent choice since many of the unifying themes of Genesis are continued in Ruth, and there are many allusions to Genesis in Ruth, ranging from direct references to characters such as Leah and Rachel to more obscure but significant allusions to Lot, Abraham, Judah, and Tamar. Just as Ruth the Moabite stumbled unaware into the field of Boaz, I had unwittingly taken on a project that was perfectly complementary to my previous work. The themes of "blessing," "seed," and "land" that were so prominent in Genesis are all found in Ruth, and a study of both Genesis and Ruth together provides a wonderful insight into the providential working of God in the fulfillment of the promises made to Abraham, Isaac, and Jacob.

Abbreviations

AB	Anchor Bible
ABD	*Anchor Bible Dictionary,* ed. D. N. Freedman. 6 vols. New York: Doubleday, 1992
BibInt	*Biblical Interpretation*
BSac	*Bibliotheca sacra*
DOTP	*Dictionary of the Old Testament: Pentateuch,* ed. T. D. Alexander and D. W. Baker. Downers Grove, IL: InterVarsity Press, 2003
ESV	English Standard Version
FCB	Feminist Companion to the Bible
HALOT	*Hebrew and Aramaic Lexicon of the Old Testament,* ed. L. Kohler et al. Trans. and ed. M. E. J. Richardson. 2 vols. Repr. Leiden: Brill, 2001
Int	*Interpretation*
JBL	*Journal of Biblical Literature*
JSOT	*Journal for the Study of the Old Testament*
JSOTsup	Journal for the Study of the Old Testament: Supplement Series
JSS	*Journal of Semitic Studies*
KJV	King James Version
LXX	Septuagint
Moffatt	James Moffatt, *A New Translation of the Bible,* rev. ed. Repr. New York: Harper & Row, 1935
NAB	New American Bible
NDBT	*New Dictionary of Biblical Theology,* ed. T. D. Alexander and B. S. Rosner. Downers Grove, IL: InterVarsity Press, 2000
NIV	New International Version
NJB	New Jerusalem Bible
NJPS	New Jewish Publication Society Version (1985)

NKJV	New King James Version
NLT	New Living Translation
NRSV	New Revised Standard Version
OBT	Overtures to Biblical Theology
OTL	Old Testament Library
RSV	Revised Standard Version
TynBul	*Tyndale Bulletin*
VT	*Vetus Testamentum*

Introduction

The book of Ruth was written originally in Hebrew. Although reading the book of Ruth meaningfully does not necessitate reading it in Hebrew, as there are many excellent modern translations, a knowledge of how dynamically and powerfully the ancient language is used will enhance the reading experience. As Ellen van Wolde points out, "The language has a dominant presence; words keep recurring, lines are spun, and a tower of images reaches up to heaven."[1] This commentary is written for English readers, and a knowledge of Hebrew is not necessary. However, throughout I will refer to the Hebrew text to enable the English reader to understand significant nuances that are not adequately conveyed by English translations. Wherever I use the Hebrew text, I transliterate and translate it.

In this Two Horizons commentary I approach the book of Ruth as Scripture and as part of the canon of Scripture. Although there are details of legal transactions in the book, the book itself is not a legal document. Consequently, some of the details about the legal transactions, particularly the marriage of Ruth, are open to different interpretations, since it was not the narrator's purpose to teach us the complex details of Israelite customs and law. In-depth discussions of the legal problems raised by the book of Ruth are provided in the technical commentaries. In this book I highlight the main hermeneutical issues in the commentary section, and I look at the broader theological implications in more detail in the second part of this book, the theological section. The raison d'être of this work is not to sort out the complex legal problems but to highlight the theological issues that are raised.

Studying Ruth as Scripture is a very rewarding project since it involves not only a study of the content of the book itself but also a study of its relation-

1. Ellen van Wolde, *Ruth and Naomi*, 3.

ship to other biblical books. In particular, the book of Ruth follows the book of Judges and precedes the books of Samuel in English Bibles, and it provides a helpful transition between these books. However, the book of Ruth also overflows with allusions to Genesis, and its theological implications become much clearer when we study it in the light of Genesis.

Although the book of Ruth is short, it has important theological implications. It is not written as a book of theology, but its narrative concerns a family history and its struggle in difficult times. The theological implications of the book relate to the faith experiences of its characters and how they understand God's dealings with them. No prophets are involved and no religious institutions are mentioned, but the book shows how faith in God sustained people in difficult circumstances and shaped their worldview. As Daniel Block points out, "The book is most eloquent in portraying the practical ethical implications of membership in the Israelite community of faith. In stark contrast to the Book of Judges, where many of the major characters are spiritually compromising at best and pagan in outlook and conduct at worst, every person in this story is a decent person; they are presented as authentic people of faith."[2] This makes the book relevant to modern readers who likewise seek to understand and conduct their lives in the light of the purposes and providence of God.

Authorship, Date, and Purpose

Ruth is an anonymous book. Although various attempts have been made to identify the author, in the absence of evidence from the book itself any attempt to discover the identity of the author is unlikely to succeed. Not only is the authorship a mystery, but there is also no clear indication about the date of the book.

Although the setting for the story is in the period of the judges, the book as we have it now was probably not written at that time. Evidence that the book was written for a later audience is found in the way that the text explains some of the practices and customs of the judges period. It is clear that the book was intended for an audience that was unfamiliar with earlier customs (see, e.g., Ruth 4:7).

Some scholars have examined the linguistic features of the book to decide whether there are any indications about the style and vocabulary that would enable us to pinpoint the date. In spite of very detailed linguistic analysis, this approach has not produced a consensus, since the evidence is ambiguous. Some

2. Daniel Block, "Ruth," 611.

archaic words used in the speeches of Boaz and Naomi may be cited in support of a preexilic date for the book, but this is not conclusive, since they may simply be a literary device that "has these older people speak in an old-fashioned way."[3] As Tamara Eskenazi and Tikva Frymer-Kensky point out, "Because these archaic forms are confined to the speeches of Naomi and Boaz, they most likely signal elevated speech and the author's indication that Naomi and Boaz belong to an older generation, cohorts in terms of age and/or status."[4] Thus the evidence in favor of an early date is not conclusive. In support of a later date scholars have cited Aramaisms in the text that they argue indicate that the text was written in the Persian period, when the use of the Aramaic language was widespread. However, we do not have sufficient evidence to pinpoint a particular date or period on the basis of Aramaisms since we do not have conclusive evidence about when these words were first used. Thus we must conclude with D. R. G. Beattie that to date the book of Ruth on "the basis of its language has proved difficult."[5] For further study of the linguistic data, consult the detailed analysis provided by Frederic Bush.[6]

Another important debate relates to the purpose of the book, which could have a bearing on when the book was written. A popular theory is that the book of Ruth was written to present a more sympathetic view of foreign women than that presented by the books of Ezra and Nehemiah. If this is correct, it would follow that Ruth was written in the postexilic era. I will discuss this theory in the theological section of this book. On the other hand, if the purpose was to support King David by showing that his choice as king was part of God's providential plan, then a much earlier date is required.

The uncertainty about the purpose of the book of Ruth arises because, although Ruth is a short and in some ways straightforward book, it is also ambiguous.[7] This adds to its interest and gives it a mysterious dimension. Thus we are not told whether the author felt that Elimelech was wise to travel to

---

3. D. R. G. Beattie, "Ruth, Book of," 427.

4. Tamara Cohn Eskenazi and Tikva Frymer-Kensky, *Ruth*, xvii.

5. Beattie, "Ruth, Book of," 427.

6. Frederic Bush, "Ruth," 18-30. On the basis of his linguistic analysis, Bush (30) argues that "the writer of the book of Ruth must have lived no earlier than the transition period between the SBH [Standard Biblical Hebrew] and LBH [Late Biblical Hebrew] phase of the language, i.e., the late pre-exilic to the beginning of the post-exilic era."

7. Many scholars have drawn attention to the ambiguity in the book of Ruth. In *Plotted, Shot, and Painted,* J. Cheryl Exum provides an excellent example of the different ways that Ruth may be interpreted. Ellen van Wolde, "Texts in Dialogue," 22, refers to the deliberate double entendres in the book. In relation to Boaz's ambiguous response to Ruth at the threshing floor, Barbara Green explains that "part of the ambiguity protects the surprise climax of the story" ("Plot of Ruth," 63).

Moab, and the reader is not informed about whether the deaths of the three men should be viewed as divine judgment. Ambiguity also keeps the deepest motives of the characters shrouded in mystery, and we do not know whether Naomi's silence in 1:18 when she "said no more" (ESV) showed disapproval of Ruth's choice to go with her; nor are we told if Naomi and Boaz actually meet. The episode at the threshing floor is an exquisite example of ambiguity and intrigue (3:1-15). When scholars refer to these ambiguities they are usually not implying "unclear content but rather the conscious, intentional employment of multiple levels of meaning in the narrative."[8] There is also ambiguity that was not intentional but was created by problems that have arisen during the process of textual transmission, and this is particularly significant in relation to the details of the marriage of Ruth and Boaz.

Perhaps, as Donald Leggett argues, it is best to interpret the book of Ruth as "having multiple purposes rather than in terms of one overriding purpose."[9] This means that the date of Ruth is uncertain but, thankfully, this does not affect its theological significance, which we will study in detail in the last two chapters of this book.

Genre

The book of Ruth has been classified as a short story, an idyll, a novella, and a divine comedy.[10] However, it is also important to note that many of the themes in the book relate to practical problems and issues similar to those discussed in the other biblical books that are usually classified as wisdom literature. Although the book of Ruth faces different issues than the book of Job, both books discuss problems that people face when God is silent and seems absent. Furthermore, practical issues relating to coping with hardship and dealing with those from outside the community are highlighted in the book of Ruth. There is a close connection between the way that Ruth is presented and the wisdom poem in Proverbs 31 about the ideal wife. Women in the book of Ruth are influential, industrious, and shrewd (wise). Set in the period of the judges, when "everyone did what was right in his own eyes," the book of Ruth shows true wisdom in operation when people act with loyalty and justice, not only with one another but with someone from a foreign country who is viewed as "the enemy" in the book of Judges.

8. Moshe J. Bernstein, "Two Multivalent Readings," 15.
9. Donald A. Leggett, *Levirate and Goel Institutions,* 295.
10. See the discussions in most commentaries, e.g., Bush, "Ruth," 30-47.

Story Line and Synopsis

The purpose of this section is to give a brief overview of the story line of the book of Ruth and also to highlight some of the main issues that will be discussed in detail in the commentary and in the theological section of this book.

The story told in the book of Ruth is comparatively straightforward. It focuses on the family of Elimelech and Naomi as they and their two sons embark on a journey from Israel to Moab. This unplanned and unwanted trip was occasioned by a severe famine in their hometown of Bethlehem — which in Hebrew means "the house of bread" — and the surrounding area. It was a difficult decision to leave their friends and neighbors, but the famine was unrelenting and the prospect of starvation demanded hard decisions.

The family's problems were intensified by the death of Elimelech in Moab, leaving a grieving widow and two sons. The sons married Moabite women, Orpah and Ruth, and then both sons died, leaving the three widows to fend for themselves. As this tragedy unfolds, we are left to wonder why it happened. It sounds very similar to the story of Job, but on this occasion it is Naomi who is left with nothing. In the book of Job, the reader is privy to what is happening in heaven, and this information highlights the innocence of Job. But in Naomi's case, there is no insight into God's thoughts on the matter, and the reader has to decide whether Naomi is innocent. Was the decision to leave Bethlehem a lack of faith in God, and were the tragedies that the family faced punishment for this transgression? Maybe even Naomi was not sure. Certainly many readers have acted as judge and jury and considered that she got what she deserved. Not so fast, though; it is doubtful whether she was consulted about the decision to leave Bethlehem, so if she was being punished, which I doubt, then she was being punished for the sin of her husband.

At any rate, news reached Moab that the God of Israel (the Lord, YHWH) had blessed his people and once again there was bread in Bethlehem ("the house of bread"). The decision to return was probably an easy one for Naomi. Moab was no place for an Israelite widow to try to eke out an existence. Her daughters-in-law set out to go with her. Presumably they carried their few possessions with them. The intention of Ruth and Orpah was to go to Bethlehem, but the intention of Naomi was to send them back to their Moabite families. There were probably arguments about this before they left their Moabite home; the discussion recorded is perhaps the culmination of similar discussions earlier. So far, Naomi had failed to convince Orpah and Ruth to return to their homes, and now on the road to Bethlehem she made one final attempt to persuade them to leave her so that she could go back home alone.

Both women expressed reluctance, and Naomi applied a lot of pressure.

Her argument was logical, persuasive, and depressing. She felt her hopelessness deeply and bordered on despair. Not only had she no family to rely on and no hope of raising another, but she also felt that even God was against her. Her insistence that her daughters-in-law leave her was not out of hatred for them; she admitted that they had both shown loyalty to her and to their husbands. Orpah listened to the reasonable case that Naomi made and decided to follow her mother-in-law's advice and return to her mother's house. Orpah is not censured in any way for this decision, and in the circumstances it seemed the wisest thing to do. Naomi now applied pressure on Ruth to follow her sister-in-law back to her culture, her home, and her gods. Ruth with steely determination made a speech, full of pathos and emotion, pledging herself to follow Naomi, to lodge with her, to worship her God, and even to die with her and be buried with her.

Naomi knew that it was futile to argue further, and the two of them stopped talking and walked on together. We are not told why Naomi did not want Ruth to return with her to Bethlehem. Perhaps she did not want to take responsibility for her; also Ruth was a reminder of her life in Moab, and now Naomi wanted to leave that country and all that happened there behind her. On the other hand, Naomia may have believed that there were opportunities for Ruth and Orpah among their own people. The journey to Bethlehem is not described, and they arrived there during the barley harvest. The women of the town were very surprised to see Naomi returning to Bethlehem. It had been over ten years since anyone there had seen her; the stress of those years may have shown on her complexion and deportment. Naomi confirmed her identity but begged them not to call her by her old name with its overtones of pleasantness, since all she felt was bitterness. But what about Ruth? She is not mentioned in these conversations; Naomi remained silent about the stranger who had returned with her. The reception of Ruth is not recorded, and this has led many to think that Naomi was embarrassed to have the foreign woman with her. However, this is not suggested in the text, and the silence about Ruth's welcome or lack of it effectively adds tension to the story. There is no suggestion that Naomi was not grateful to have her company. At some stage the news had spread to everyone in the town, including Boaz, that Ruth had been a source of strength to Naomi.

Ruth soon made clear that she did not intend to be a liability to her mother-in-law. Taking the initiative, she set out into the harvest field to work among people who, although not hostile to her, nevertheless recognized her as a foreigner. The text suggests that, from Ruth's point of view, it was by accident that she arrived at the field belonging to Boaz. Apparently she did not know about his relationship to Naomi nor could she have foreseen the role that he would eventually play in her life. However, what appeared to be a random choice of a place to work was evidence of God's guidance. The same God who guided Abraham's servant to the house where Rebekah lived (Gen 24) had now guided Ruth to the field of Boaz. What happened next is not entirely clear; the text is ambiguous about the exact request that Ruth made to the foreman in charge. Did she just ask for the opportunity to gather the few kernels of grain that escaped from the harvesters, or was her request more daring, going beyond what the foreman could possibly grant? In the commentary I will consider the two main ways that the text can be understood, but here I shall assume that Ruth asked permission to glean and this was granted.

Later that morning Ruth was exhausted; she had no access to the water and food provided for the workers. A shelter for the workers had been erected on the site to provide an escape from the blistering heat of the sun, and she took the liberty of resting there. Ruth was the only one resting at that time because the others were aware that the owner of the field was arriving. Boaz arrived and exchanged the customary greetings, but he noticed one person whom he had not seen before. What was this woman, this stranger, doing in his workers' shelter?

Boaz summoned his foreman and asked him about whom the stranger belonged to, assuming perhaps that she was related to one of his workers. The foreman's answer was careful and defensive. He identified Ruth as the woman who had returned from Moab with Naomi. She had requested permission to glean and had been working steadily except for this short break that she was now taking. With this information, Boaz approached Ruth. We can imagine her unease as this man, who she now realized was the owner of the field, approached. However, he addressed her endearingly as "my daughter," and not only made clear that she was welcome in his field but also insisted that she should not go to any other field. He also assured her that if she stayed close to his female workers she would be safe since he had instructed the men not to touch her. Furthermore, he gave her permission to avail herself of the supply of water. This acceptance and generosity amazed Ruth, and consequently her first words to Boaz express her bewilderment that someone like him should show so much generosity and concern to a foreigner. Boaz indicated that he had heard a great deal about Ruth. His short speech is important because it indicates that Naomi must have told others how much she appreciated Ruth's company. The information that Boaz had received commended Ruth for leaving her own country and kindred to care for Naomi, and this information could only have come from the elderly woman herself. Following a further expression of gratitude from Ruth, Boaz invited her to join the harvesters for a meal. He gave her so much that there was enough left over to take home to Naomi. The harvesters were instructed to allow her to glean unimpeded wherever she wanted and that they should even drop some grain on purpose for her to pick up.

The story of Ruth's return to Naomi is a wonderful example of the narrator's ability to make the reader feel part of the drama and to communicate the inner emotions of the characters. Slowly the story unfolds as Ruth arrives at Naomi's house carrying an impressive supply of grain. First we are told that Naomi saw the grain, and the skillful narrator allows us to appreciate her surprise — this was beyond her expectations. But then Ruth revealed another surprise as she uncovered the portion of roasted grain that she had kept over from mealtime after she had eaten her fill. This generous supply of food led Naomi to ask about the location of the field that Ruth had gleaned in, and before Ruth could answer she blessed the unknown beneficiary who had shown such generosity. Now at last, with tension in the story increasing with each word, Ruth revealed the identity of the man who had treated her so well — it was none other than Boaz. Naomi, who arrived home bitter, now exploded with emotion and relief. "May he be blessed by the LORD, whose kindness has not forsaken the living or the dead!" (Ruth 2:20 ESV).

However, this outburst is ambiguous; it is not entirely clear whose kindness she referred to — that of Boaz or YHWH? If the subject of her praise is YHWH, which I think is likely, then this is a turning point in the book when the old woman's faith is rekindled and the bitterness against her God is beginning to dissipate. Following a disclosure to Ruth about the status of Boaz as their near relative and a potential redeemer, Ruth revealed that Boaz had invited her to stay with his harvesters. Significantly, Ruth used the male form for "harvesters," implying that Boaz had given her permission to accompany the male harvesters, whereas Boaz had specifically used the female form and had clearly instructed her to stay close to his female workers. Now Naomi picked up Boaz's warning and repeated it. It would be much safer for Ruth if she stayed with the women — these were the lawless days of the judges, after all.

By going out to glean each day Ruth was able to provide for her mother-in-law and herself throughout the harvest period. In chapter 3 it is Naomi's turn to plan for their survival. She could see beyond the harvest time, and she was not lulled into complacency by the availability of food in the short term. Knowing that the harvest would soon end, she sought to provide a longer-term solution. It could be considered a daring plan, born out of desperation and fraught with risk. However, perhaps Naomi's knowledge of the character of Boaz meant that it was less risky than if a complete stranger had been involved. There is a clear parallel with the Genesis story of Tamar, who was forced to take desperate measures because of the inactivity of Judah (Gen 38:12-19). In the case of Tamar, Judah had failed to keep his obligations; and in the case of Ruth, Boaz had initially shown much interest and generosity but had failed to follow this up. Boaz's lack of initiative reminds one of Barak in the book of Judges, who needed a little push from a woman to overcome his reticence (Judg 4:6-9).

At any rate, Naomi concocted the daring plan, and it fell to Ruth to carry it out. This involved careful preparation, including different clothes and a furtive visit to the harvest field at night. Timing was all-important according to Naomi, and so Ruth kept Boaz under surveillance until he had eaten and drunk. Ruth probably depended on her new clothes to provide the required anonymity while she waited in the distance for Boaz to finally lie down and succumb to sleep. At midnight she made her move and quietly went to where he was sleeping, uncovered his feet, and lay down. Now she had fulfilled Naomi's plan, and the rest depended on Boaz. "Who are you?" asked the startled man as he awakened to find a woman at his feet. The stranger identified herself as his servant Ruth. Now at this stage Ruth had fulfilled all Naomi's instructions, but the young woman with tremendous courage went further. Rather than waiting for Boaz to tell her what to do, she told him what to do. Thus unexpectedly Boaz found himself propositioned at midnight by this foreign woman, not only to marry her but also to provide for Naomi by redeeming the land that belonged to Elimelech, her late husband. Boaz's reply was everything she could have hoped for, except that he revealed that there was yet another potential redeemer who must be given the first opportunity to redeem the land.

Ruth lay on the threshing floor until just before dawn. Boaz was anxious that she should leave before anyone would see her. He supplied her with six measures of grain so that she would not return to Naomi empty-handed. The night had not produced all that Naomi had hoped for, but at least there was something to show for this daring exploit. When Ruth entered the house, Naomi asked the same question that Boaz had asked several hours earlier: "Who are you?" (Ruth 3:16; see, e.g., KJV). Many translators think that this question is out of place here since Naomi knew who she was, but perhaps the question was more subtle and meant, "Who are you now — still the foreign woman, or a rich man's wife?"

Having done their part, the two women must now leave matters in the hands of the men, who meet at the city gate. That is how things happen in a patriarchal society: the women work, plan, and raise the families while the men make all the decisions. The place for decision was at the city gate — an area at the entrance to the town where people could congregate and hold discussions, and where even court proceedings could take place. Boaz lost no time in setting up a meeting at the city gate, where he accosted the other redeemer in the presence of witnesses. The second redeemer was addressed as פְּלֹנִי אַלְמֹנִי/*pĕlōnî 'almōnî* in the Hebrew text. This was not his name and is best translated "So-and-So." The man's real name has been lost or deliberately obscured.

The business took place in two stages. First, Boaz revealed to the other redeemer that an opportunity had arisen to buy the land that belonged to Elimelech from his widow. Without hesitation, the man accepted the offer. What happened next is debatable. According to the majority of English versions, Boaz informed the redeemer that if he bought the land he must also marry Ruth. However, this detail is taken from the margin of the Hebrew text; the text itself suggests that Boaz informed the man that he (Boaz) intended to marry Ruth. Both options have problems, which I will discuss in the commentary and in the theological section of this book.

Whichever way we understand the story, the effect is the same: the redeemer was no longer willing to buy the land since the additional information he had now received suggested that there would be complications regarding his children's inheritance. The deal was confirmed when So-and-So removed his sandal and gave it to Boaz. This symbolic action was the equivalent of signing a legal document, and it signified the relinquishing of his right to the land.

The story now reached its denouement with the marriage of Ruth to Boaz and the birth of a baby. Although it was Ruth's baby, the women of Bethlehem congratulated Naomi. The once bitter woman had found fulfillment and security through her daughter-in-law and through this new baby. The book of Ruth concludes with a short genealogy that shows the significant role played by this baby — Obed, the grandfather of King David.

The story of Ruth is about women, but the genealogy is entirely about men.

Outline

Commentary

1:1-5 From Bethlehem to Moab

Succinctly and clearly, the opening verses of Ruth transport the reader to a bygone era when the judges ruled in the land of Israel.[1] Our use of the term "judge" today has little relevance in this context since these judges were not court officials or judicial professionals but military heroes. Their primary role was to provide protection from the enemy and avenge Israel when others treated them unfairly. Justice in Israel had strong practical overtones. For example, when Isaiah called for justice he exhorted people to "correct oppression; bring justice to the fatherless, plead the widow's cause" (Isa 1:17 ESV). These judges were defenders of the people against those who oppressed them. However, even ancient heroes could not solve all the nation's problems, and they could not prevent drought and famine. Moreover, although some Israelites would later idealize the time before the monarchy and regard them as the "good old days," those days were characterized by violence and lawlessness (Judg 21:25). Although the lawlessness of the period of the judges is not prominent in the book of Ruth, there is just a hint of it when both Boaz and Naomi mention the possibility of Ruth being molested in the harvest field (Ruth 2:9, 22). However, the story of Ruth is not about violence but about love and commitment: the love of people for each other and the love of God that ignores national boundaries.

The book of Ruth opens on a discordant note. The land inhabited by Abraham's descendants[2] and the land described to Moses as "a land flowing with milk and honey" (Exod 3:8, 17) was now in the grip of a severe famine,

---

1. Literally the Hebrew reads, "In the days when the judges judged."
2. God had promised that Abraham and his offspring would be greatly blessed if Abraham left his homeland and went to the land that YHWH would show him (Gen 12:1-3).

probably caused by drought. Many questions are raised by this famine: Was it punishment from God or a result of mismanagement or the result of enemy activity? We can ask these questions, but it is not the purpose of the book of Ruth to answer them. Although the story of Ruth is set in the context of a famine, the famine is not the subject of the book. However, this famine provides the reason for the departure of a Hebrew family from Bethlehem ("house of bread") to the neighboring country of Moab, which lay east of the Dead Sea. Although Moab was not far from Bethlehem, conditions in Moab were sometimes different; it was possible to have rain in Moab but none in Bethlehem.[3] We may assume that there were some communications between Bethlehem and Moab since the family would need reassurance that their journey would be worthwhile. Presumably news had reached Bethlehem that times were much better in Moab, just as in Jacob's time news had reached Canaan that "there was grain for sale in Egypt" (Gen 42:1 ESV).

There was probably a well-established route to Moab crossing the Jordan just north of the Dead Sea, and a number of families may have traveled in that direction to escape the famine. However, our story relates to just one of these families, that of Elimelech and Naomi with their two sons, Mahlon and Kilion.

The aim of Elimelech and his family was "to live for a while in the country of Moab" (Ruth 1:1 NIV). Although the NIV translation ("to live for a while") gives the impression that they only intended to stay for a short time, the Hebrew verb גור/*gûr* can refer to short- or longer-term residence. Its most frequent use is in relation to dwelling with strangers, and nowhere is this more pertinent than in Isa 11:6, where the wolf dwells (*gûr*) with the lamb. The noun גֵּר/*gēr* occurs frequently in the OT and refers to a sojourner or alien (Gen 15:13; Exod 12:48; Lev 19:33). Both the noun and the verb refer to the status of the person concerned rather than to a particular period of time. Although there is no indication of how long Elimelech intended to stay in Moab, it is likely that he anticipated returning to Bethlehem when the famine was over since apparently he still owned land there (Ruth 4:3).

The versions describe their stay in different ways: the KJV has "continued there," ESV "remained there," and NIV "lived there" (1:2). These different translations reflect the simple Hebrew statement, וַיִּהְיוּ־שָׁם/*wayyihyû šām*, "they were there." This does not suggest that they stayed longer than expected and is not a negative comment.

The names of the family are interesting. "Elimelech" refers to the concept of divine kingship. It may be translated "My God is king" or "God is king," and it reflects the period of the judges when Israel was not governed by kings, but

---

3. This point is made by Edward F. Campbell Jr., *Ruth,* 50-51.

the national deity YHWH was worshiped as their king. Elimelech is the first name in the book of Ruth, and the last name is David, a human king who would recognize that he was subservient to YHWH and exercise leadership under his authority.

As we are told later in the book, the name "Naomi" conveys the idea of pleasantness. The names of the two sons were Mahlon and Kilion. The names rhyme in Hebrew and, as Jack Sasson points out, this is not uncommon in the OT: Uz the firstborn, Buz his brother (Gen 22:21), Muppim and Huppim (Gen 46:21).[4] There have been lengthy discussions about the significance of the names Mahlon and Kilion. "Mahlon" possibly conveyed the idea of "sickly," but we cannot be certain. "Kilion" may have suggested "to be finished." Taken together the meanings of the names may be something like "Weakening and Pining."[5] However, Edward Campbell is correct when he comments that we "simply do not yet know" the meaning of these names.[6]

The family is described as Ephrathites. The meaning of the description "Ephrathite" is not entirely clear. Perhaps Ephrath/Ephrathah was a district that included Bethlehem, or perhaps it was another name for Bethlehem itself. But Ephrathah was the name of Caleb's wife, and one of her descendants, Salma, is described as "the father of Bethlehem" (1 Chr 2:50-51). Therefore, as Robert Hubbard points out, Ephrathite may be the name of their clan and it may indicate that Elimelech was from an aristocratic family.[7] If indeed Elimelech was from a wealthy and influential family, it highlights the greatness of the tragedy that deprived him and his family of all they had acquired. However, the most important detail about the term "Ephrathite" is that King David is described as "the son of an Ephrathite of Bethlehem" (1 Sam 17:12). Thus at the very start of the story we are already given a hint of its conclusion with the birth of David's grandfather.

The question arises about whether the decision to move to Moab was a good one. Some commentators are very critical, as was rabbinic tradition. As Sasson explains,

> Elimelech, it was taught, was punished either because of extreme avarice or because he forsook the Holy Land; he should have stayed put to alleviate its difficulties in time of drought. As to the untimely deaths of Mahlon and

---

4. Jack M. Sasson, *Ruth*, 18. Sasson also mentions Hemdan and Esban, and Yitran and Keran (Gen 36:26).

5. See ibid., 19. Sasson also points out that midrashic commentators favor "Blot out and Perish" for Mahlon and Kilion, respectively.

6. Campbell, *Ruth*, 54.

7. Robert L. Hubbard Jr., *Ruth*, 91.

Kilion, recounted in verse 5, it was clear to rabbis that these two were punished for marrying non-Jews. In addition, all three were eternally punished by being buried in Moab.[8]

Elimelech's decision to take his family to Moab would not have been taken lightly. Not only was travel difficult but also finding acceptance in a foreign country would have been a tremendous challenge. The problems related to remaining in Judah must have greatly outweighed the difficulties involved in moving to Moab. We must assume that families who remained in Bethlehem at that time faced starvation. In leaving Judah, Elimelech was following the example of Abraham and Jacob, who left Canaan and went to Egypt because of famine (Gen 12:10; 46:1). The choice of Moab rather than Egypt was probably made for practical reasons since Moab was closer than Egypt, and during the period of the judges, especially after the defeat of Eglon, Moab may have been at peace with Israel (Judg 3:30).

Elimelech's death is stated without comment, and the book does not suggest that this was punishment for leaving Judah. Comparison with the story about Judah's children in Genesis would suggest that if death was brought about by the judgment of God this would be indicated in the text. Note the clarity in the following verse from Genesis: "But Er, Judah's firstborn, was wicked in the sight of the LORD, and the LORD put him to death" (Gen 38:7 NRSV). There is nothing similar to this in the book of Ruth, and Elimelech's death is recorded as a natural event. Anyhow, the purpose and message of the book are not focused on Elimelech, and very little information is given about his life and death in Moab: we do not know how he died, how old he was, or how long he had been in Moab. The focus of the book is on returning to Judah rather than on the reasons for leaving it. The main story is not about Elimelech but about Naomi, Ruth, and Boaz.

Although the journey to Moab was necessary at the time, Elimelech probably hoped to take his family back to Judah and reclaim his land. There are parallels here with the account in Genesis of Jacob taking his family to Egypt during a famine. Jacob died in Egypt, but even at the end of his life he did not lose sight of returning to Canaan, and he was buried in that land (Gen 49:29). It was one of those heartrending family tragedies that Elimelech, like Jacob, did not live long enough to make that return journey; he was buried in Moab since his widow and sons did not have the resources to repatriate his body to Bethlehem.

Marriage took place between the two sons of Naomi and two local women; Mahlon married Ruth, and his brother Kilion married Orpah. Scholars have

---

8. Sasson, *Ruth,* 20.

discussed at length the meaning of the women's names but have not agreed on a definitive explanation. Certainly the name Ruth sounds similar to a word for "friendship," but the spelling is different (רוּת/*rût* and רְעוּת/*rĕ'ût,* respectively). Since assonance was often more important than etymology in Hebrew names, this suggestion is still tenable, though Daniel Block describes it as "wishful thinking."[9] The name Orpah has been connected to words meaning "perfume" or "nape of the neck." The idea that her name meant "nape of the neck" has been linked to her turning back to Moab. However, this implies that Orpah was not her original name but was given to her after her "turning back" to Moab. As Frederic Bush points out, an etymology of the name Orpah that relates to her turning back is often used to suggest that her name is fictional and was "invented to fit her role in the story."[10] However, if the narrator was inventing names with specific meanings, the names chosen and their meanings would probably have been much more obvious. Orpah may have been a Moabite name whose meaning we do not know. Jewish tradition, however, built on the idea that her name meant "one who turned back," and the Midrash added to this that she became the ancestress of the Philistine warrior Goliath![11] There is no evidence for this; it represents an attempt to blame Orpah for her decision. As we shall see below, this is something that the text does not do.

Marriage to foreign women is sometimes frowned upon or even condemned in the OT, because intermarriage usually involved accepting not just the foreign wife but her gods as well. The dangers of intermarriage are exemplified by Solomon; he not only married a large number of foreign women but also built temples for their gods and even worshiped them (1 Kgs 11:1-8). However, in a number of cases foreign marriages are not explicitly condemned: Abraham married Keturah after Sarah's death (Gen 25:1); Joseph married the daughter of an Egyptian high priest (Gen 41:45); Moses married the daughter of the priest of Midian (Exod 2:21); and Esther married King Xerxes (Esth 2:17). Mahlon and Kilion are not condemned for their choice of wives, and it is clear that the behavior of both women was exemplary (see Ruth 1:8). They stayed in Moab for about ten years. Ten years also recalls the period that Abraham and Sarah had waited for children before taking matters into their own hands in the debacle that led to the birth of Ishmael (Gen 16:1-3).

The mention of ten years without children indicates that this was a further problem that the family faced. It was not only one marriage without children but two! The problem of barrenness is highlighted in Genesis not only in rela-

---

9. Block, "Ruth," 587.
10. Bush, "Ruth," 65.
11. L. Rabinowitz, *Midrash Rabbah: Ruth,* 2:20 (p. 38).

tion to Abraham and Sarah; the marriage of Isaac and Rebekah also faced this problem. In each case the problem of barrenness is carefully developed in order to present the important theological truth that children are a gift from God. This same message is presented in the book of Ruth as it ends with the birth of Obed, showing that God was in control throughout and that he had planned this significant birth and enabled it to happen (Ruth 4:18-22).

When it seemed that things could not get any worse, tragedy struck again: Mahlon and Kilion died. Like the death of Elimelech, their deaths are mentioned succinctly and in a matter-of-fact manner. Unlike the story of Judah's family, these deaths are not described as divine judgment (cf. Gen 38:6-10). As in the case of Elimelech, this lack of information about the circumstances of these deaths serves to shift our attention fairly quickly onto the main characters of the drama — Naomi and her daughters-in-law. Naomi's bereavement first of her husband and then of her two sons is reminiscent of the story of Job. Like Job, Naomi lost those who were near and dear to her, and the future seemed bleak indeed. The loss of her husband followed by the death of both sons was a disaster of catastrophic proportions, and it was greatly exacerbated by the sense of loneliness that she would have felt since she was away from her closest friends and acquaintances. There were almost certainly no social structures in Moab designed to protect foreign widows or to provide for them. The pathos of the passage is deepened by the term used in the text to describe the two sons who died. In v. 5 the word יְלָדִים/*yĕlādîm* is translated "sons," whereas in v. 3 בָּנִים/*bānîm*, the usual word for "sons," is used. The former usually refers to children; it is very unusual for this term to refer to married men. However, it helps to convey the depth of Naomi's loss since, even though they were married, Mahlon and Kilion were still her boys — her children. The word יֶלֶד/*yeled* will be used also at the end of the book with reference to the child of Ruth and Boaz. The new baby represented a new beginning for Naomi, but he also represented a continuation of the line of descendants that she had assumed had become extinct with the death of her two sons.

Thus the book of Ruth commences with an account of unexplained tragedies that came in quick succession to Elimelech's family. The absence of any explanation in the book of Ruth about why this family should suffer so much is one of the strengths of the story because it relates well to life as we know it; we do not always have answers when things go wrong. Death left this family stunned, without answers, and this impression is conveyed in the powerful rhetoric of the biblical text that leaves the reader, like the family, without an explanation.[12]

---

12. Hubbard comments that the narrator "leaves the stunned reader pondering unanswerable questions" (*Ruth*, 92).

My understanding of the book of Ruth avoids trying to blame Elimelech or his family and refuses to see their tragedies as punishment. However, one should note that Jewish tradition took a very different approach. The Targum (the Aramaic version of Ruth) declares unequivocally that Elimelech sinned in going to Moab and was punished by death. His two sons disobeyed God by marrying foreign women and they also suffered accordingly (1:5).[13] There is a similar emphasis in the Midrash, which, as Campbell observes, portrays God as patiently "seeking to produce repentance in them by a series of warnings across the ten years before their ultimate retribution."[14]

If the author intended us to read the tragedies at the beginning of the book as punishment, why did the author not make this clear? Either the author did not believe that these deaths were punishment, or the author felt that the questions should be left open — just like sad events in life. I believe that the book deliberately avoids pointing the finger of blame at the family, and we should accept this as the context of the story. Certainly Naomi does not mention anything about being punished by God for sin. This of course does not preclude that she must have been troubled by many regrets about leaving Bethlehem. Danna Fewell and David Gunn, for example, imaginatively paint the following scenario to describe how Naomi may have felt after her husband and sons died:

> She knew they should never have come. It had been wrong from the beginning. Leaving their own folk, their native place, to live among these foreigners. Elimelech's death, the barrenness, now the deaths of her sons, both of them. They should all have gone back years ago when she had heard that the famine was over. The boys should never have married Moabite women. They should have gone back home to find wives.[15]

This interpretation is reasonable since Naomi obviously had many doubts and regrets. However, there is no suggestion that she was being punished by God for the decision to leave Bethlehem. If she had felt that the family was guilty, we should have expected this admission from her, but she simply blamed God for her calamity, not her husband or children. Furthermore, in a patriarchal society it is possible that she was not consulted by her husband about the decision to leave Bethlehem, just as the text makes no mention that Abraham consulted Sarah about the decision to leave Haran (Gen 12), or even the divine command to sacrifice Isaac (22:1-19).

---

13. Étan Levine, *Aramaic Version of Ruth*, 20.
14. Campbell, *Ruth*, 58.
15. Danna Nolan Fewell and David Miller Gunn, *Compromising Redemption*, 26-27.

1:6-7 Naomi Prepares to Return to Bethlehem

Naomi heard news in Moab that YHWH had visited his people. The Hebrew of v. 6 clearly emphasizes the phrase "the country of Moab," which occurs twice. This repetition is not obvious in some translations (e.g., NIV), but the RSV shows it clearly: "Then she started with her daughters-in-law to return from the country of Moab, for she had heard in the country of Moab that the LORD had visited his people and given them food" (cf. also NRSV, KJV). Why is the reference to Moab repeated here when the reader has already been informed that Naomi is in Moab? Repetition is usually not accidental in Hebrew literature; it is used to highlight the key event or theme in a passage. The narrator on several occasions uses the same word twice to draw attention to the importance of that particular moment or to emphasize a particular aspect of the book's message. Repetition draws the reader's attention to important details that might otherwise be missed. In this verse the repetition highlights the interesting fact that what YHWH has done in Israel has become well known in Moab. Thus what has happened in Israel has been so dramatic that it is newsworthy elsewhere — even in Moab, which had its own deity, Chemosh. Moreover, what Naomi hears is that YHWH has visited *his* people. When God blessed his people, the Israelites, they acknowledged that their change in fortunes were not just good luck but the result of the direct intervention of God in their affairs.

What had YHWH done? He "had visited his people and given them food" (ESV). Israelites did not believe that God was remote and detached from history. They believed that if they obeyed and honored him, he would "visit" them, bringing blessing and victory. The Hebrew word פָּקַד/*pāqad* has a different nuance from the English "visit." The Hebrew word conveys the idea of a powerful and dramatic visitation that would change their situation. When God "visits" people, he makes a difference to them and to their situation. For example, before his death in Egypt, Joseph reassured his family that God would "visit" them and bring them back to the land promised to the patriarchs (Gen 50:24-25). When God "visited" his people it was a wonderful reminder that he had not forgotten his promises. The biblical text does not suggest any reason why YHWH had visited his people at that particular time, but the Aramaic version of Ruth states that it was in answer to the prayers of Boaz (Targum of Ruth 1:6; 3:7).[16] While there is no evidence of this in the biblical text of Ruth, it is appropriate for the period of the judges in which the story is set. According to the book of Judges, times of prosperity and peace came in response to repentance and spiritual renewal.

---

16. Levine, *Aramaic Version of Ruth*, 50, 88.

This account of YHWH coming to the aid of his people is reminiscent of what happened in exile when Israelites were permitted to return to their distant homeland to rebuild the temple. There was an acknowledgment that "the LORD has done great things for them." This is illustrated clearly in Ps 126:1-2, where the joyful reaction of the Israelites to their release from captivity evokes a response from people of other nations: "When the LORD brought back the captives to Zion, we were like men who dreamed. Our mouths were filled with laughter, our tongues with songs of joy. Then it was said among the nations, 'The LORD has done great things for them'" (NIV). A significant aspect of Israel's faith as expressed in the OT was the confidence that, even when the nation faced disaster, their God was able to respond to their need and provide deliverance and blessing.

The news that God had blessed the people in Bethlehem with food encouraged Naomi to make the decision to leave Moab. Apparently, the home in Moab was sold or abandoned, and all three women began walking toward the land of Canaan. Ruth 1:7 implies that the initial intention was for all three to go to Bethlehem, and they were probably carrying all their possessions.

1:8-13 An Emotional Farewell as Naomi Leaves Moab

However, somewhere on the journey Naomi stopped and explained to her daughters-in-law that they should not continue with her any further. We do not know how far they had gone at this stage, but both Ruth and Orpah apparently assumed that they would be going to Bethlehem with their mother-in-law. We are not told whether Naomi had discussed the situation with them previously. Perhaps if the women had understood that she intended to return to Bethlehem alone, they would have pressured her to stay in Moab. However, at some stage on the journey she strongly advised them to go no farther. This may have come as a great shock to them. Where would they go and how would they survive? It was a momentous decision that Naomi was urging them to make.

Her prayer is that YHWH would show "kindness" (חֶסֶד/*ḥesed*) to them as they had shown to her and the dead. This shows that Naomi believed that YHWH's jurisdiction extended to Moab and that his activity was not confined to the land of Israel. Thus her understanding of YHWH's jurisdiction is unlimited by political borders. With our developed theological understanding and our knowledge of not only the OT but also the NT, we take for granted the universal jurisdiction of YHWH. However, in the polytheistic world of early Israel, many assumed that each deity was limited to a specific territory. Thus when the Syrian leper Naaman was healed, he asked for two mules loaded with Israelite earth so that he could worship Israel's God, even in Syria (2 Kgs 5:17). Naaman's request shows that he understood YHWH as a local deity who could be worshiped only on his own territory. Naomi's vision of God was much greater; she believed that his dominion extended outside the borders of Israel. It is not reading too much between the lines to suggest that this may have been her personal experience. Like Jacob and Joseph in Genesis, she may have experienced YHWH's presence in a foreign country, and she believed that it was appropriate to express the hope that YHWH would continue to deal faithfully with her two daughters-in-law even though she assumed that they were staying in Moab.

Although most versions translate *hesed* as "kindness," this does not convey adequately the meaning of this important OT word in this particular context. The women had been faithful and caring during times of sickness and bereavement; in this context, as in many others, "steadfast love" is a better translation. Naomi made clear that she had no complaints about the two foreign women. Both Ruth and Orpah had been steadfast in showing love to their husbands and to Naomi herself. The reference here is not just to the emotional aspects of love but also to its practical outworking. During their time of marriage, and probably throughout periods of illness, the women had been faithful and steadfast in their commitment. Naomi hoped that YHWH would reward them for their faithfulness and show them steadfast love.[17] As Edward Campbell observes, *hesed* is "more than ordinary human loyalty; it imitates the divine initiative which comes without being deserved."[18] Evidence that *hesed* is a characteristic of YHWH is found throughout the OT (Gen 39:21; Exod 20:6; 34:6; Num 14:18; Deut 5:10; Neh 9:17; Pss 25:10; 62:12; 86:5). It is a virtue that YHWH demanded from his people but did not always receive (Hos 6:4). However, Naomi commends both Orpah and Ruth for showing this desirable quality to their husbands and to her.

Naomi's hope and wish for the women was that YHWH would grant that they "may find rest" (Ruth 1:9). The noun translated "rest" (מְנוּחָה/*mĕnûḥâ*) occurs just over twenty times in the OT. It refers to a place to camp after a journey (Num 10:33), and it describes the land that God had promised his people (Deut 12:9). It is also used in Ps 23:2 in the context of "the still waters" or "waters of rest" to which the shepherd leads his flock. As Hubbard observes, the word "connotes permanence, settlement, security, and freedom from anxiety after wandering, uncertainty, and pain."[19] Naomi had very fixed ideas about how a woman could acquire such rest. Influenced by her knowledge of the patri-

17. Sasson argues that Naomi felt in debt to the two women and, since she could not repay that herself, "Naomi was asking her own god, Yahweh, to fulfill such an obligation, at least until the girls find happiness in newer marriages" (*Ruth*, 23).

18. Campbell, *Ruth*, 81.

19. Hubbard, *Ruth*, 105.

archal societies in which she had spent all her life, she believed that the only way a woman could find rest was to find a husband. This meant that she felt personally that there could be no "rest" for her since she was too old to find another husband. Bordering on despair herself, she wanted the very best for her daughters-in-law. However, in her desire for them to have "rest" is the implicit complaint that this will not happen for her.

At first Orpah and Ruth both resolutely expressed the desire to go with Naomi to her people. Naomi asks, "why will you go with me?" (Ruth 1:11 NRSV). We do not know why Naomi argued so strongly that the women should not go with her. Perhaps she was aware of the difficulty involved in finding husbands for two Moabite women in Israel and did not want that responsibility. On the other hand, it may have been the women's future welfare and security that were uppermost in her mind, and therefore she wanted them to stay in Moab and marry again. With cold but convincing logic, Naomi made clear to them what they must have already realized: she had no more sons to give them and no possibility of arranging marriages for them (1:9-12). Naomi pointed out that she had no prospects of marrying again, and even if she did and then had sons, the two women would not be able to wait until they grew up in order to marry them. Therefore, according to Naomi, there was no future for Ruth and Orpah if they stayed with her, and they must return to their "mother's house." It is interesting that she refers to their mothers and not to their fathers. As Leon Morris points out, this is a reminder that this book is "written from a woman's point of view."[20] In the parallel story in Genesis, Tamar returns to her "father's house" (Gen 38:11).[21] I discuss the interesting phrase "mother's house" in detail in the theological section of this book.

Naomi's attempt to prevent the women from going with her was a very unselfish approach since her journey from Moab to Canaan would be hazardous and lonely. She was willing to travel alone rather than take the women with her into an uncertain future. Perhaps there is also the suggestion that if they had gone with her they would have been dependent on her and she felt unable to cope with this responsibility. Moreover, Naomi may have worried about the reception that a Moabite woman would have received in Bethlehem. Whatever the reason, Naomi was determined to go back to Bethlehem alone. She was unaware at that time that there was hope for the future and that her hope lay with one of the women whom she was trying to dissuade from going with her.

20. Leon Morris, "Ruth," 253.

21. Some early versions had a problem with this reference to the women returning each to her mother's house. Codex Alexandrinus has "father's house" and the Syriac has "parents' house" (see Jan de Waard and Eugene Nida, *Translator's Handbook on Ruth*, 12, 84 n. 24).

Explaining her situation to the two women and the consequent reminder of her own hopelessness caused Naomi to be bitter and to blame YHWH. "The hand of the LORD has gone out against me" (1:13 ESV). When the "hand of the LORD" is mentioned in the OT, it usually refers to God's judgment against Israel's enemies (Exod 6:1; 7:5; Deut 5:15; 26:8). Naomi believed that YHWH had become her enemy. She did not blame misfortune, fate, or bad luck. She was convinced that God had acted against her decisively and harmfully. It was not just that she thought that God was not helping her; it was worse than that — God was against her. Job had similar thoughts, and many other biblical characters went through dark periods of feeling forsaken by God; Elijah and Jeremiah are good examples (1 Kgs 19:4; Jer 12:1-4; 15:18). Psalm 44:18-24 (ESV) also reflects a time of struggle and spiritual confusion.

> Our heart has not turned back,
> > nor have our steps departed from your way;
> yet you have broken us in the place of jackals
> > and covered us with the shadow of death.
> If we had forgotten the name of our God
> > or spread out our hands to a foreign god,
> would not God discover this?
> > For he knows the secrets of the heart.
> Yet for your sake we are killed all the day long;
> > we are regarded as sheep to be slaughtered.
>
> Awake! Why are you sleeping, O Lord?
> > Rouse yourself! Do not reject us forever!
> Why do you hide your face?
> > Why do you forget our affliction and oppression?

In the NT the cross is the most poignant example of an occasion when the question "Why?" rang out in the darkest hour, "My God, my God, why have you forsaken me?" (Matt 27:46).

However, Naomi seems to have gone beyond asking "Why?" She had reached a stage of sad acceptance and bitterness. The exact meaning of her words in the second part of v. 13 is not entirely clear; two different translations of the following clause are possible. The Hebrew is: כִּי־מַר־לִי מְאֹד מִכֶּם/*kî-mar-lî mě'ōd mikkem*, literally, "Bitter to me very from you." The different ways of understanding the clause can be seen by a comparison between the NIV and ESV. "It is more bitter for me than for you" (NIV) or "it is exceedingly bitter to me for your sake" (ESV).

Either translation is possible; but in this context, where she is complaining about the way that the Lord has dealt with her, the NIV translation, which emphasizes her bitterness, is probably correct. Hubbard provides his own translation, and he succeeds in teasing out the nuances implicit in the text, "For I am in far more bitter straits than you are."[22] This conveys a feeling of self-pity bordering on despair, which is understandable in the circumstances. Although the women have suffered, they have hope because they are young; but for Naomi there is only a sense of hopelessness.

1:14-18 The Difficult Decision Facing Ruth and Orpah

Naomi's persistence and logic finally persuaded Orpah to kiss her mother-in-law goodbye and to make a new start in Moab (1:14). As she walked away from Naomi and Ruth, she also walked out of our story and is not referred to again.[23] As soon as Orpah left, Naomi tried again to persuade Ruth to do likewise; she pointed out that Orpah had returned to "her people and to her gods." As Hubbard observed, although the Hebrew word אֱלֹהִים/*'ĕlōhîm* suggests several deities, "the reference is surely to the Moabite god Chemosh."[24] The mention of the Moabite god at this juncture highlights the choice that Ruth must make. It is not just a choice between Judah and Moab or between Naomi and her mother; it is also a choice between Chemosh and YHWH.

In spite of Orpah's departure and Naomi's logical arguments, Ruth continued to cling to her. The Hebrew verb "to cling" is דָּבַק/*dābaq*. This verb is used in situations where a very close relationship is involved, such as that between husband and wife (Gen 2:24). It is also used in the context of a close relationship with God (Deut 10:20; 11:22; 30:20; Josh 22:5; 2 Kgs 18:6).

Ruth's decision is surprising because there was no obvious advantage in following Naomi. Her mother-in-law was not wealthy, and her tragic circumstances were weighing heavily on her. She was overcome with grief, and being in her company would be demanding and stressful. However, in spite of all the adverse circumstances and uncertainty, Ruth was determined to accompany Naomi into an unknown future with no guarantee of a happy ending. Perhaps she just could not tolerate the idea of her mother-in-law making that dangerous

---

22. Hubbard, *Ruth*, 112.

23. Phyllis Trible observes, "Orpah is a paradigm of the sane and reasonable; she acts according to the structures and customs of society. Her decision is sound, sensible, and secure. Nevertheless, Orpah dies to the story. However commendable her way, it is not the dynamic of the tale" (*God and Rhetoric*, 172).

24. Hubbard, *Ruth*, 116.

journey on her own. Whatever motivated Ruth, it is clear that love and concern for Naomi were important factors in her decision. It is more difficult to ascertain what role the God of Israel played in her thinking at this stage. She showed knowledge of Naomi's God and referred to him as "the LORD" (YHWH), and she was prepared to declare that "your God will be my God." Although this does not amount to a declaration of personal faith, it does highlight that leaving behind the god of Moab was not problematic for her. It is impossible to know what fears lurked in her heart and mind as she made her decision, but it seems clear that love overcame all the possible reasons for not staying with her mother-in-law. Her words have become immortalized as an expression of love and selfless commitment.

> But Ruth said, "Do not urge me to leave you or to return from following you. For where you go I will go, and where you lodge I will lodge. Your people shall be my people, and your God my God. Where you die I will die, and there will I be buried. May the LORD do so to me and more also if anything but death parts me from you." (Ruth 1:16-17 ESV)

Repetition is employed to great effect in this famous statement of commitment. The Hebrew rhetoric is concise and powerful, and it is not possible to translate it without losing something of the dynamic beauty of the statement. For example, a literal rendering of the Hebrew in the third sentence is: "your people, my people; your God, my God." The Hebrew is more concise than the English since only one Hebrew word is required to convey each of these possessive statements. Nevertheless, even in English, this is one of the most beautiful and selfless statements in the Bible. Ruth's statement of commitment is unequivocal and total. She will never return to Moab but will go with her mother-in-law and die in her country and be buried there. André LaCocque makes an interesting comparison between Ruth and her ancestor Lot. Ruth's determination to leave her homeland contrasts with the reluctance of Lot and his family to leave Sodom (Gen 19:14-22). That event ended tragically when Lot's wife looked back and became a pillar of salt (Gen 19:26). In contrast, Ruth was resolute that she would never turn back.[25] Another important contrast between Ruth and Lot is that Abraham's nephew showed no reluctance to leave his uncle. On the contrary, he was so attracted by the lush scenery in the Jordan Valley that he needed no persuasion to go in that direction (Gen 13:10-11). Sadly this was also taking him toward Sodom and trouble. Lot followed what was attractive in his eyes, but Ruth was persuaded by the loyalty and love in her heart.

25. André LaCocque, *Ruth,* 53.

In Ruth's speech she declared, "where you lodge, I will lodge." Campbell understands this reference to lodging to refer to the journey to Bethlehem.[26] However, Sasson argues convincingly that Ruth is not referring to the journey home but to the future. Ruth will be content to stay with Naomi for the rest of her life, whether in a palace or a hovel. The use of the verb "to lodge" (לין/*lûn*), with its temporary connotation, suggests that "Ruth was willing to share with Naomi an unsettled future, so long as nothing parted them."[27] Bush agrees with Sasson that it is not just the journey to Bethlehem that Ruth is referring to, and he points out helpfully that the contrast between the verbs "to go" and "to lodge" creates a merism. This grammatical term describes the use of two opposite terms to embrace everything between. Thus "all who go out and all who come in" is a merism for "everyone." In this case Bush suggests that the contrast between "to go" and "to lodge" really means "all of life."[28]

The intensity of Ruth's commitment is emphasized by the reference to death and burial. These are important themes in the OT, and in the ancient world generally much thought and often great expense were involved in how and where people were buried. The first significant claim to land in Genesis by a patriarch was the purchase of Machpelah by Abraham to bury his wife Sarah, and Abraham himself was also buried there (Gen 23:19; 25:9). When Jacob went to Egypt, it was particularly important for him that he not be buried there (49:30). This showed that his commitment was to Canaan, not to Egypt. Even Joseph, who at one stage was totally assimilated into Egyptian society, asked that his bones one day be buried in Canaan (50:25). In contrast to the patriarchs, Ruth's desire to be buried with Naomi was a statement of total commitment. Although she was born in Moab, she would not be buried there.

The text also suggests that Ruth's commitment was not just a matter of loyalty to Naomi but also included faith in Naomi's God. The statement that Naomi had made, blaming YHWH for her troubles, had not deterred Ruth. Thus she expressed her determination to stay with Naomi by making an oath in the name of YHWH. She showed no allegiance to Chemosh and invoked only the name of YHWH in a way that suggests that he was her God.[29] Ruth could have used the more general term for "God," but instead she used the name YHWH. Yael Ziegler contends that this is particularly significant: "Many scholars note that Ruth's deliberate decision to employ the name of the LORD, rather than the general usage of the name of God, underscores her active and

---

26. Campbell, *Ruth*, 74.

27. Sasson, *Ruth*, 30.

28. Bush, "Ruth," 82.

29. Morris comments that Ruth has "taken Yahweh to be her God and it is upon Him accordingly that she calls" ("Ruth," 261).

total acceptance of the personal God of Israel. At the same time, it is a deliberate and conscious rejection of any other god."[30]

Ruth's reference to YHWH was not the first time that a foreign woman acknowledged Israel's God; Rahab had done this when she addressed the spies and acknowledged that everyone in Jericho knew that YHWH had given the land to the Israelites (Josh 2:9-12). However, whereas Rahab asked the spies to take an oath, it is Ruth herself who confirms her commitment by an oath, her use of the name YHWH increasing its significance. An oath was a particularly strong form of speech. It may originally have been associated with elaborate ceremonies such as that described in Genesis 15, where Abraham cut the animals and birds into pieces. This became the setting for a solemn covenant that YHWH made with him. Campbell suggests that whereas Ruth did not perform such an elaborate ceremony, she may have alluded to such practices with a symbolic gesture "something like our index figure across the throat."[31] This, of course, is conjecture. The closest parallel to this oath is in 1 Sam 20:13, where Jonathan assures his friend David that he will warn him if his father Saul intends to harm him: "But should it please my father to do you harm, the LORD do so to Jonathan and more also if I do not disclose it to you and send you away, that you may go in safety" (1 Sam 20:13 ESV). These oaths are assurances of commitment and loyalty to a close friend, and both invoke the name of YHWH. Usually the name invoked in such oaths was Elohim; therefore, as Campbell points out, "there is a purpose for this shift from the basic form, in that there is an important emphasis on Yahweh in these passages."[32]

There is a difference of opinion about the translation of the last part of Ruth's oath. Most translations have "if anything but death" separates us (ESV, NIV, KJV, NJB, NJPS). Bush supports this translation: "Ruth is swearing that death alone will separate her from Naomi."[33] However, the phrase may also be translated "if even death parts me from you" (NRSV). If this translation is correct, it suggests that even in death they shall not be separated. Thus, as Campbell suggests, "Ruth's final and climactic sentence promises loyalty to death and to the grave."[34]

The Hebrew version of Ruth leaves the faith of Ruth somewhat ambiguous, but the Targum, reflecting later Jewish tradition, is much more forthright and declares that Ruth received instruction in Israelite religion from Naomi and became a proselyte.

---

30. Yael Ziegler, "So Shall God Do," 79.
31. Campbell, *Ruth*, 74.
32. Ibid.
33. Bush, "Ruth," 82.
34. Campbell, *Ruth*, 75.

But Ruth said, "Do not urge me to leave you, to turn back and not to follow you; for I demand to be converted." Naomi said, "We are commanded to observe the Sabbaths and Holy Days, not to walk more than two thousand cubits." Ruth replied, "Wherever you go, I shall go." Naomi said, "We are commanded not to dwell together with the nations." Ruth replied, "Wherever you dwell, I shall dwell." Naomi said, "We are commanded to observe six hundred and thirteen commandments." Ruth replied, "Whatever your people observes, I shall observe, as though they were my people originally." Naomi said, "We are commanded not to engage in idolatry." Ruth replied, "Your God is my God." Naomi said, "We have four death penalties for the guilty: the throwing of a stone, burning by fire, death by the sword, and hanging on a tree." Ruth replied, "However you die, I shall die." Naomi said, "We have two cemeteries." Ruth replied, "And there I will be buried. And do not continue to speak. Thus and more may the Lord do to me, if anything other than death shall separate us." (1:16-17)[35]

The religious interests of the Aramaic version are clear and contrast with the simplicity of the Hebrew version, in which the innermost beliefs and fears of Ruth are not revealed. It was abundantly clear, however, that Ruth showed such intense determination that Naomi realized that it was pointless to argue any more (Ruth 1:18).[36] The English might be misunderstood here and interpreted as stubbornness on Ruth's part. However, the Hebrew root translated "determined" (אמץ/'ms) does not usually convey the idea of a stubborn determination but rather has overtones of bravery and commitment (cf. Josh 1:6). Ruth was bravely making a choice that would change her life, and she was resolute and unequivocal.

Thus the strength of Ruth's statement persuaded Naomi that it was pointless to argue any more. She obviously did not agree with this decision but accepted it because of Ruth's determination. Naomi's reaction is that "she said no more" (Ruth 1:18 ESV). This clause could be translated literally as "she stopped talking to her." Some scholars interpret this clause as implying silent withdrawal and seek to understand why Naomi would have reacted in this way. As Fewell and Gunn observe, Naomi "speaks not a word either to, or about, Ruth, from this point to the end of the scene in the arrival at Bethlehem. If Ruth's famous 'Where you go, I go; your god, my god' speech can melt the hearts of a myriad

---

35. Levine, *Aramaic Version of Ruth*, 22-24, 56-62.

36. Kirsten Nielsen argues that the lack of a response from Naomi to Ruth's expression of commitment "creates a tension in the story that leads the reader to ask how this unusual relationship can possibly develop" (*Ruth*, 50).

preachers and congregations down the centuries, why not Naomi's heart?"[37] Naomi's silence could be interpreted as reflecting her self-centeredness. She may have been so overwhelmed by her own problems that she failed to empathize with others or to appreciate the selfless commitment of Ruth. On the other hand, her silence may betray her fear of the future, not just for herself but also for Ruth, since she knew that a foreign woman might not receive a warm welcome in Bethlehem.

The statement that Naomi "said no more" has also been interpreted as an expression of annoyance. Fewell and Gunn argue that Naomi is very annoyed that Ruth is coming with her and resents her presence: "Naomi is attempting to shake free of Moab and the calamity that she associates with that place and its people. Resentment, irritation, frustration, unease may well lie behind her silence. Ruth the Moabite may even menace her future."[38] A similar approach is taken by Katherine Doob Sakenfeld, who points out that Ruth would be a constant reminder to Naomi of the tragedies that had happened in Moab, and she suggests that Naomi may have been able to hide the foreign marriages of her sons if she had returned alone.[39] Naomi may also have been very annoyed at Ruth's decision because she felt that it was a mistake. She may have been deeply concerned for Ruth and very upset that she was losing a good opportunity to start again. Perhaps in Naomi's view Ruth was throwing her life away and would live to regret it. However, Kristin Saxegaard warns against reading too much into the silence of Naomi. She contends that there is "no reason in reading a catfight into the narrative," but suggests that "Naomi in her self-pity, just does not take much notice of Ruth."[40]

Moreover, the reference to Naomi's silence does not necessarily mean that she stopped talking to Ruth completely, but it could imply that she stopped talking to Ruth about the subject of her return to Moab and that she gave up trying to persuade her to return. Possibly she was glad of the company, and anyhow she was absolved from any responsibility and could not be accused of persuading Ruth to go with her. The details of long journeys are not usually recorded unless they have a direct bearing on the main story line (cf. Gen 12:5).

Ruth and Orpah, faced with the same situation, made different decisions. Orpah returned to her family and presumably to the worship of Chemosh (the god of Moab). Ruth's choice to accompany Naomi meant that she would worship YHWH, not Chemosh. Naomi's testimony in this time of trouble had

---

37. Fewell and Gunn, "Son Is Born to Naomi," 100.
38. Fewell and Gunn, *Compromising Redemption,* 74.
39. Katherine Doob Sakenfeld, *Ruth,* 35.
40. Kristin Moen Saxegaard, *Character Complexity,* 103.

been very negative, and she had blamed YHWH for her troubles, but this did not deter Ruth, who probably had observed the family faith in more positive times. This comparison between Ruth and Orpah is reminiscent of Genesis, where two people are frequently compared and one is chosen for blessing, for example, Cain and Abel (Gen 4:4-5), Shem and Ham (9:26-27), Abram and Lot (13:14-18), Isaac and Ishmael (17:19-21), Jacob and Esau (28:13-15), Judah and Joseph (49:22-26; cf. 1 Chr 5:1-2). In this case Ruth is highlighted as making the wise choice, though this was not apparent at the time. The choice that she made set her life on a new course, whereas Orpah returned to her family and her god and we never hear about her again. Orpah is not criticized in the text or represented as being selfish.[41] She becomes a foil for Ruth, not because her actions were evil or ill considered but because she made the logical choice that most people would have made in the circumstances. Orpah had been a good wife to Kilion, and Naomi commended her for loyalty. As Campbell observes, "Orpah is a worthy woman," and "we are invited to look at the extraordinary in Ruth, not focus on some imagined failure in Orpah."[42] Ruth's choice is remarkable because it is out of the ordinary and represents a most unusual step of loyalty and bravery. Ruth's commitment is all the more remarkable because of the lack of encouragement that she received from Naomi. Ruth's decision to care for her mother-in-law was not only a selfless decision but also, at least at this stage, a thankless one.

Sakenfeld draws attention to ways that the book of Ruth should not be used, and she wisely points out that "we must be cautious about generalizing Ruth's words to her mother-in-law as a desirable model for all women." Ruth's commitment to her mother-in-law was voluntary and cannot be cited as the normally accepted behavior. Sakenfeld is aware of situations where a daughter-in-law was expected to be "the virtual servant of her husband's parents."[43] To use the book of Ruth to support burdening someone with a commitment that they did not earlier envisage is a misuse of Scripture.

Although we have been focusing on Ruth's commitment and selfless decision, we get a slightly different perspective when we read the book of Ruth in the light of the main themes in other OT books. A recurring theme in Genesis is that God sometimes chooses the most unlikely people. The firstborn, who would have been expected to be the most prominent member in a family's history, was often ignored, and even characters like Jacob, who was somewhat

---

41. Sakenfeld points out that the contrast between Orpah and Ruth does not imply "a negative judgment" about Orpah's behavior since she was the one who actually "followed Naomi's instructions" (*Ruth*, 30).

42. Campbell, *Ruth*, 82.

43. Sakenfeld, *Ruth*, 34.

devious, were chosen and blessed. This theme continues in the books of Samuel, where even David, who was to become the great king of Israel, was not considered a likely candidate — when Jesse assembled his sons before Samuel, he did not even invite David (1 Sam 16:11). It need not surprise us, then, that some of his ancestors were also unlikely candidates for the roles that they played. Others underestimated David, but God chose him; and this important theme — that God uses unlikely people — is highlighted by the choice of a Moabite woman to be his great-grandmother.[44]

Jewish tradition draws attention to the fact that Naomi tried to dissuade Ruth three times, and then she realized that she had fulfilled her responsibility. Ruth's determination was shown by her persistence. She had ample opportunity to change her mind. If after three times Ruth still insisted, then this was proof of her resolve. This significance of three refusals was adopted by Jewish thought in relation to proselytes. This is explained in the Midrash: "Three times is it written here 'turn back,' corresponding to the three times that a would-be proselyte is repulsed; but if he persists after that, he is accepted."[45] This comment reflects the idea that the repeated refusal would test the sincerity of the would-be proselyte. Jesus used a similar technique when he asked Peter three times if he loved him. By asking Peter to repeat his loyalty three times, Jesus was testing his resolve and also reminding him of his threefold denial (John 21:15-19).

1:19-22 Ruth and Naomi Arrive in Bethlehem

The journey between Moab and Bethlehem is not described. This is not unusual; even the long journey that Abraham took from Babylon to Canaan is not described in detail. It is the destination that is important, not how they got there. As they entered Bethlehem, the two travelers became the focus of attention.

> So the two of them went on until they came to Bethlehem. And when they came to Bethlehem, the whole town was stirred because of them. And the women said, "Is this Naomi?" (Ruth 1:19 ESV)

It is not surprising that it is the women who asked this question. The women probably knew Naomi much better than the men. Their question may suggest incredulity and shock. Perhaps ten years in Moab with much hardship and

---

44. Eugene Merrill observes that God "seems to take delight in using the foreign, the frail, and perhaps even the disreputable to accomplish His eternal purposes" ("Book of Ruth," 138).

45. Rabinowitz, *Midrash Rabbah, Ruth* 2:16 (p. 36).

sorrow had taken their toll, and they could scarcely recognize Naomi. This is the view of the Midrash, which seeks to explain the question, "Is this Naomi?" by embellishing the story:

> In the past she used to go in a litter, and now she walks barefoot, and you say "Is this Naomi?" In the past she wore a cloak of fine wool, and now she is clothed in rags, and you say, "Is this Naomi?" Before her countenance was ruddy from abundance of food and drink, and now it is sickly from hunger, and yet you say, "Is this Naomi?"[46]

However, it is more likely that the reaction from the women of Bethlehem should be understood positively. This is the view of Campbell: the "reaction is certainly one more of delight than of pity."[47] Taking a similar approach, Bush describes the reaction of the women as "delighted excitement." According to Bush, the rhetorical question "Is this Naomi?" arises not because of "Naomi's aged and careworn condition," but it "expresses surprise and delighted recognition."[48] Ten years had elapsed since any of the women had seen Naomi, and they probably had given up hope that she would return. Now unexpectedly she walks into the town during harvest and her name is suddenly on everyone's lips with a reaction of both surprise and delight. Thus the phrase, "the whole town was stirred because of them" (1:19 ESV), reflects the excitement of those who had not seen Naomi for a decade. This view is supported by other occurrences of the verb הום/*hûm*, "to stir."[49] For example, in 1 Sam 4:5 this verb is used in the context of the great excitement that occurred when the ark of the covenant was brought into the Israelite camp: "As soon as the ark of the covenant of the LORD came into the camp, all Israel gave a mighty shout, so that the earth resounded [*hwm*]" (ESV). If we take this as analogous (see also 1 Kgs 1:45), it suggests that all Bethlehem was in a state of joyful excitement and the news of Naomi's return was on everyone's lips, causing a noisy atmosphere of surprise and celebration.

Naomi, however, could not join in the excitement or hide her disappointment at how her life had unfolded. She reacted against everyone's delight to see her. The reunion with friends could not alleviate her feelings of forsakenness. At the mention of her name with its connotation of "pleasantness," Naomi took the opportunity to pour out her heart to the women of Bethlehem. Rather than providing her with a reason for celebration, Naomi's return to her homeland became

46. Ibid., 3:6 (p. 47).
47. Campbell, *Ruth,* 75.
48. Bush, "Ruth," 92.
49. According to *HALOT* 1:242, the root could also be המם/*hmm*.

the setting for a strong and bitter complaint against her God, who she believed had treated her badly. The reader has encountered a previous complaint from Naomi made in Moab in which she referred to her life as "bitter." The long journey to Bethlehem and the sight of the harvest field had done nothing to cheer or hearten her. Indeed, her return to Bethlehem had given her even more reason for bitterness as the once familiar scenes brought back memories of happier times. Even the mention of her name on the lips of the women of Bethlehem caused her to complain that her name should be changed from "pleasant" to "bitter," thus reflecting her innermost feelings and her miserable circumstances: "She said to them, 'Do not call me Naomi; call me Mara, for the Almighty has dealt very bitterly with me'" (Ruth 1:20 ESV). Naomi's response includes a wordplay on the theme of bitterness: קְרֶאןָ לִי מָרָא כִּי־הֵמַר שַׁדַּי לִי מְאֹד/*qěre'nā lî mārā' kî-hēmar šadday lî mě'ōd*. This wordplay is very difficult to reproduce in English. Moffatt tried to do this with: "Call me Mara, for the Almighty has cruelly marred me." Naomi's previous complaint mentioned the bitterness of her life, but now in Bethlehem she goes further and complains that the Almighty (Shaddai) has caused her to be bitter. Job made a similar complaint claiming that the Almighty (Shaddai) has made his soul bitter (Job 27:2).

Apparently, "Shaddai" was an ancient name for God. In his conversation with Moses, God explained, "I appeared to Abraham, to Isaac, and to Jacob, as God Almighty [El Shaddai], but by my name the LORD [YHWH] I did not make myself known to them" (Exod 6:3 ESV). The origins of this name are not entirely clear, but it is usually translated as "Almighty," and when prefixed by El, "God Almighty." Bush observes that the name occurs "in passages involving blessing and cursing (cf., e.g., Gen 17:1; 28:3; 35:11; Num 24:4, 16 . . .)." He also notes that it occurs "frequently in contexts expressing judgment (e.g., Isa 13:6; Joel 1:15; Job 5:17) and power (e.g., Ezek 1:24; 10:5; Pss 68:14; 91:1)."[50] The use of this particular name conveys Naomi's depth of despair. If it is the Almighty who has dealt bitterly with her, who can come to her aid? Also by using such a name she suggests that God is powerful and able to help her but has refused to do so. Naomi feels that the one who is able to do great things for his people has done nothing for her.

The second part of Naomi's complaint explained that she felt not only bitter but also "empty" (Ruth 1:21). The Hebrew word order of Naomi's complaint clearly emphasizes the words "full" and "empty." To duplicate the effect that the text conveys in Hebrew we could translate: "Full I went away, and empty YHWH brought me back." Her sense of emptiness probably related to the absence of her husband and two sons. She did not seem to derive much comfort

---

50. Bush, "Ruth," 92-93.

from the presence of Ruth. As this story proceeds and reaches its denouement, the readers will be assured that Naomi had not been forgotten and that indeed God had a plan for her life. However, Naomi's speech has one positive aspect. She acknowledged that YHWH had brought her back. Even in bitterness and disappointment she still had a deep awareness of God in her life. Naomi never even hinted at atheism. Her problem was not that God did not exist; she believed that he existed but that he was not helping her.

Although we do not know when the book of Ruth was written, we can surmise that some of the readers of this book would be in exile or diaspora, and it is likely that Naomi's complaint about God would find an echo in their hearts: if Israel's God was El Shaddai, then why had he not rescued his people? Earlier stories of "homecoming" in Genesis and Exodus had been very different — Abraham had returned from Egypt after a famine with much wealth; and Jacob, who left home alone and without possessions, returned with wives, children, and wealth. Naomi, in contrast, had nothing except a daughter-in-law whose company she had not welcomed. It is interesting that the word מָרָא/ *mārā'*, "bitter," also occurs in the exodus story (Exod 15:22-25). In that context the reference is to the people's complaint about bitter water, but YHWH made the bitter water sweet. Eventually he would also remove Naomi's deeply felt bitterness and restore the sweetness and pleasantness that the meaning of her name conveyed.

In the midst of her gloom and disappointment, Naomi suggested that her name should be changed. Names were significant, and a change of name was usually associated with an important change in circumstances. Name changes were particularly significant in the book of Genesis; the names of Abram, Sarai, and Jacob were changed by God to reflect their new relationship with him (Gen 17:5, 15; 32:28). Naomi wanted her name changed because it did not reflect her experience. YHWH had brought calamity upon her. It is unusual that someone should deliberately choose a name that was linked with trouble, since most people feared the power of a name to bring trouble upon them. There is one incident in the Bible where a person was worried that his name would bring him trouble. His name — Jabez — reflected the word for "pain." His mother gave him this name because of the pain she suffered during his birth (1 Chr 4:9). He was worried that because his name was related to pain that he would experience much pain during his life. He prayed for deliverance from the consequences of this bad name, and his prayer was answered (1 Chr 4:10). However, Naomi was not afraid of the name change to "bitter" since, from her perspective, the worst tragedies imaginable had already befallen her.

Verse 21 ends with a strong statement from Naomi that may be translated in different ways: לָמָּה תִקְרֶאנָה לִי נָעֳמִי וַיהוה עָנָה בִי וְשַׁדַּי הֵרַע לִי/*lāmmâ tiqre'nâ lî noʿŏmî wyhwh ʿānâ bî wĕšadday hēraʿ lî.* Ambiguity about the verb *ʿānâ* has led to two possible translations. Depending on the context, the verb can be translated "to humble" or "to answer." Thus it is not entirely clear whether we should translate v. 21 as "The Lord has dealt harshly with me" (NRSV) or "The Lord has testified against me" (ESV). Either translation is possible, but there is no doubt about Naomi's overall sense of despair since she was convinced that she was the victim of injustice and calamity. To make matters worse, she believed that it was YHWH who was afflicting her, and it was the Almighty (Shaddai) who had brought about her calamity.

As Hubbard observes, she "lays the blame for her miserable fate directly at Yahweh's door."[51] This is a reaction that many of the early readers of the book of Ruth may have been able to identify with, since Israel's history was punctuated by catastrophes such as famine, locust plagues, earthquakes, and enemy activity that threatened their very existence. In such circumstances, Naomi's accusation that God was not helping her but was indeed working against her may have found an echo in the hearts of others facing disaster. Indeed, readers who had been forced into exile and who had faced the collapse of all that they believed important would have found it very difficult not to question why God had forsaken them (see Lam 5:20).

Naomi's sense of emptiness was also a reflection of her negative attitude to the presence of Ruth. She did not consider it a blessing to have Ruth with her, and the presence of her daughter-in-law did nothing to allay her fears or take away her feeling of despair and emptiness. Perhaps Naomi thought of Ruth as an additional burden — someone else to worry about — rather than the one through whom her needs would be met. The impact of Naomi's attitude to her own emptiness and her lack of understanding how Ruth could solve their problems is that at this stage she had no idea of how things would work and could only expect the worst.

She had heard that God "had visited his people." However, this sense of blessedness had not made her personal lot any easier to bear. God may have visited his people but he had not visited her. It is interesting that the person she had reluctantly brought with her from Moab would be used by God to bring personal blessing to Naomi, but any such hope was far from her mind at this stage. Is this self-pity or a chance once again to share with her own people the sort of inner emotion that foreigners in Moab would not have understood? Was Naomi glad to be among her own people again, with whom she could unburden her heart and share her pain?

Although she was apparently unconscious of God working for her benefit,

---

51. Hubbard, "Naomi's Shrewdness," 284.

this is what was happening at that time. Others in the Bible had a similar sense of abandonment. Thus Gideon expressed his frustration with the following question addressed to the angel, "And Gideon said to him, 'Please, sir, if the LORD is with us, why then has all this happened to us? And where are all his wonderful deeds that our fathers recounted to us?'" (Judg 6:13 ESV). Gideon's conclusion was that God had abandoned them, and Naomi seemed to be overwhelmed by a similar sense of disillusionment and Godforsakenness.

In contrast to Naomi's personal sense of loss and abandonment, we are told that they arrived at the beginning of the barley harvest.[52] YHWH had indeed visited his people. They were harvesting grain and baking bread in Bethlehem. This would not have made it any easier for Naomi to see God blessing others while she was not benefiting personally. Other people were harvesting crops, but her husband had owned land there, and, in different circumstances, he too would have been busy bringing in the harvest. But he and her sons were dead and their land was unproductive and unattended. Naomi's sense of despair was too overwhelming to hide.

Thus the first chapter concludes with a brief statement summarizing the most important detail of the story so far: "So Naomi returned, and Ruth the Moabite her daughter-in-law with her, who returned from the country of Moab. And they came to Bethlehem at the beginning of barley harvest" (Ruth 1:22 ESV). This summary statement may seem unnecessary to the English reader, but it is highly significant in that it draws our attention to one of the main themes of the book — returning to Israel. The verb שׁוּב/*šûb*, "to return," occurs twelve times in this chapter. This theme of returning to Canaan is also very prominent in the book of Genesis and is another indication of the continuation of Genesis themes in the books that follow it. The Hebrew of Ruth 1:22 states that Naomi returns and then repeats the same verb with Ruth as subject. This repetition is very significant since it means that Ruth did not just come to Bethlehem in the company of Naomi but that she personally returned in her own right. As Bush points out, the narrator gives Ruth's return "remarkable prominence."[53] This emphasis is particularly strange since Ruth has not been in Judah before. Indeed, of the three women, Ruth is the only one who had not "returned home": Orpah returned to her mother and Naomi returned to Bethlehem, but Ruth has turned her back on her home in Moab. However, the narrator makes clear that Ruth also has "returned home." Are we meant to understand this in a spiritual sense? LaCocque points out that the verb not only indicates a physical

---

52. As Brian Britt observes, "The phrase 'barley harvest' (קציר שׂערים) appears only twice in the Hebrew Bible: 2 Sam. 21:9-10 and Ruth 1:22" ("Death, Social Conflict," 2).

53. Bush, "Ruth," 94.

return "but also repentance." According to LaCocque, Ruth's movement can be described as "return" because she "turns her back on the plains of Moab; she repents of the ancestral sin."[54] Murray Gow makes a similar point, arguing that although Ruth "had not previously been to Judah," by entering the community of Israel "to whose God she has given her allegiance," Ruth indeed in a sense "has come to her true home." Gow also comments, "The word שׁוב *(to return)* may be regarded very much as a theme word of Ruth 1, and it is not impossible that it is endowed here with a religious nuance as well as its secular sense, so that there is more than just a journey to Bethlehem but rather a return to the embrace of the covenant community."[55]

The repetition of this idea of "returning" is a significant indication not only of the interests of the author, but also of the situation of many of the first readers of the book. It is interesting to surmise that if Israelites in exile and diaspora had access to this book, it may have been a source of encouragement. It is possible that many Israelites in diaspora would have been able to identify with Ruth since like her they would not have been to Israel before — they would have been born in exile. Even so, by making that decision to go to Judah, they would in a very real sense be "returning home."

2:1-3 Introduction to Boaz and Ruth's Initiative

The introduction to Boaz is slightly confusing due to two possible readings. It is not entirely clear whether Boaz is introduced as a relative (Qere) of Elimelech or simply as a friend (Ketib).[56] Most translations prefer "kinsman," but Hubbard prefers "friend."[57] The reader should therefore keep an open mind about whether Boaz is introduced as a relative or as an acquaintance. Either interpretation is possible.

The introduction to Boaz is brief and succinct. The only information given is that he is from the family of Elimelech. We are not given any meaning

---

54. LaCocque, *Ruth,* 34.

55. Murray D. Gow, *Book of Ruth,* 101 and n. 8.

56. John Barton provides the following helpful explanation: "The Masoretic text of the Hebrew Bible records two parallel versions of the sacred texts: the scribal version, and the version which was known through the tradition of oral recitation. The device of *qere* and *kethibh* is the method by which these two 'texts' can be recorded through a single written text. The marginal *qere* registers those places where the traditional recited version of the text would suggest a different set of graphic signs from those that actually appear in the text transmitted by scribal tradition, and registered in the body of the written Hebrew text" (*Spirit and Letter,* 123-24).

57. Hubbard, *Ruth,* 132-33.

for his name, but it sounds like Hebrew words that could be interpreted as, "In him is strength."[58] Boaz is not a common name; he shares it with one of the pillars of the temple, which, of course, was not built until the time of King Solomon (1 Kgs 7:21). Some have suggested that Solomon named one of the pillars in memory of Boaz, who was one of Israel's most honored ancestors.[59] This suggestion is supported by the way he is described in the text: אִישׁ גִּבּוֹר חַיִל/ *'îš gibbôr ḥayil,* literally, "a man, mighty of strength." This connection between this man of strength and the temple pillar is an interesting suggestion, but one that must remain a conjecture because of the absence of evidence.

However, "a man, mighty of strength," is only one of a number of possible translations, as modern versions indicate, for example: "worthy man" (ESV), "prominent kinsman" (NAB), "prominent rich man" (NRSV), "man of standing" (NIV). Although we do not have evidence to link Boaz to a character mentioned in the book of Judges, as Sasson points out, "Rabbinic commentators, in general, identified Boaz with Ibzan of Bethlehem" (Judg 12:8-10).[60] However, there are no grounds for this identification in either Judges or Ruth.

Having introduced Boaz, the narrator returns to Ruth and Naomi. Ruth asks Naomi for permission to go to the harvest fields to glean. In a society without any social services for the poor and vulnerable to rely on, there were rules to protect the poor. Gleaning was one of the provisions for those in need, including resident aliens. They were permitted to follow the harvesters and pick up the occasional stalks that were dropped accidentally (Deut 24:21). Landowners were instructed not to harvest to the edge of their land so that something would be left for the poor and the alien to glean (Lev 19:9-10; 23:22). Ruth's request that she be permitted to glean shows her willingness to help and to submit to her mother-in-law's authority. On the other hand, it suggests that Ruth was not being badgered by Naomi to provide for them both, although clearly it was either not possible or not appropriate for Naomi herself to glean. The relationship between the two women seems to have been cordial and characterized by mutual respect.

Clearly, however, it is Ruth who takes the initiative. She had shown strength and resolve when she decided to go to Bethlehem with Naomi, and now this same strength of character is reflected in her refusal to be inactive as she ventured out alone into an unfamiliar situation to seek help from people she did not know. Naomi simply acquiesced and gave permission to Ruth to go

---

58. On the other hand, as Nielsen points out, D. R. G. Beattie "interprets it through the Arabic verb meaning 'to be shrewd'" (*Ruth,* 54, referring to Beattie, "Ruth III," 46).

59. See the useful discussion about the name "Boaz" in Hubbard, *Ruth,* 134-35.

60. Sasson, *Ruth,* 15.

and glean. The reader already knows about Boaz, but Ruth did not know him; and, surprisingly, Naomi did not inform her.

Ruth is referred to as "Ruth the Moabite" (2:2), and readers can be forgiven for thinking that this is unnecessary since her nationality has been made clear. However, this emphasizes that she is a foreigner seeking favor from Israelite harvesters. Foreigners were not always welcome in the close-knit societies of the ancient Near East, and Moab and Israel, even at an early stage, had a history of conflict. On the other hand, Israelite law and practice were apparently very favorable toward strangers and the poor. It was a reflection of YHWH's own concern for those who were vulnerable and needy (Lev 23:22).

The reference to "the field" is to a large cultivated area of farmland situated outside the town. It was not divided by hedges or walls, but each person's piece of land was marked by boundary stones. Ruth did not know about Boaz and simply happened upon his part of the harvest "field" as if "by chance" (Ruth 2:3). The NJPS brings out the meaning of the Hebrew clearly: "as luck would have it, it was the piece of land belonging to Boaz." However, the perceptive reader is aware that this is not the entire story.[61] From Ruth's point of view she has found the right field by chance, but the reader is aware that God is working out his purposes in this situation. As Sasson comments,

> The labeling of Ruth's meeting with Boaz as "chance" is nothing more that the author's way of saying that no human intent was involved. For Ruth and Boaz it was an accident, but not for God. The tenor of the whole story makes it clear that the narrator sees God's hand throughout. . . . By calling this meeting an accident, the writer enables himself subtly to point out that even the "accidental" is directed by God.[62]

Ruth was unaware that she had been guided to the right place. It could not have occurred to her that Israel's God was guiding her. Why would God be interested in her? The powerful message of this text is that although Israel's God is separate and lofty (Exod 15:11-18), he is also the one who cares about the individual and in particular who takes the part of the oppressed. Another good example is the story told in Genesis about Hagar. Her owners Sarah and Abraham treated this woman deplorably, but God took an interest in her, protected her, provided for her, and gave her a purpose and a future (Gen 16–21). In the same way, in this story God guided the helpless woman to the person who could provide for her. It may have seemed like a piece of "good luck" to Ruth, but behind the so-called

---

61. Trible comments, "Within human luck is divine intentionality" (*God and Rhetoric*, 176).
62. Ronald Hals, *Theology of the Book of Ruth*, 11-12; quoted by Sasson, *Ruth*, 44.

luck was the gracious hand of God working out his own purposes through the life of this foreign woman. There are also parallels between the situation of Ruth and that of young Samuel, who was unaware that God was speaking to him because his experience was still very limited, but God protected him and "let none of his words fall to the ground" (1 Sam 3:19 ESV).

This contrast between perceptions of what is a blessing and what is merely good luck is still pertinent in our modern world. What one person may see as "blessing," another without the benefit of faith will just treat as "good luck." In a person's outlook on life, "faith" changes "luck" into "blessing," and "coincidence" into "providence."

2:4-7 Boaz Arrives at the Harvest Field

When Ruth arrived at the area being harvested by Boaz, he himself was absent, but she requested permission from the foreman to glean and began to work (Ruth 2:3). The account gathers momentum with the arrival of Boaz. He greeted his harvesters in the name of YHWH and they responded in kind. Did this greeting and the response it received carry special significance? People often use greetings without stopping to consider the meaning of the words that they have used. For example, the English greeting "goodbye" is from the Old English "God be with you." However, it is very doubtful if the majority of people who use this greeting are even aware of its origins. Such greetings do not convey a religious meaning and are simply long-established formulae that people have become so familiar with that they no longer consider the content of the greeting or its religious meaning. Perhaps this greeting and its content should be considered as simply an insignificant formula that Boaz and the reapers were accustomed to using. On the other hand, we have seen that our narrator is very concise and does not provide extraneous information. If the greeting was simply a record of the fact that Boaz said "Hello" to his workers and they replied "Hello" to him, then it is very doubtful if the narrator would have bothered to mention this detail. Furthermore, blessing is a recurring theme in the book of Ruth. In the light of this, Sakenfeld suggests that "Boaz's greeting should be read with its full theological meaning."[63] Therefore, the prominence of this greeting and its content may indicate that it is a significant indication of the community's faith. It may mean that Boaz and the workers recognized that the task of harvesting a crop was a special privilege because their recollection of famine and failed crops was still vivid.

63. Sakenfeld, *Ruth*, 41.

Hubbard highlights another interesting aspect of the greeting: its chiastic structure and its response. The greeting commences with the name of Israel's God, YHWH, and the response ends with this special name.[64] Using "this simple device" of the greeting, "the narrator reminded his audience that, though offstage, Yahweh was nevertheless within earshot."[65] A similar acknowledgment that a bountiful harvest is evidence of YHWH's blessing is found in Genesis 26, where, after a time of famine, Isaac reaped a bountiful harvest.

The theme of blessing is also important in the context of relations between Israel and Moab. Before Israel's entrance into Canaan, the king of Moab, in an attempt to subdue Israel, summoned a prophet to curse them (Num 22:5-6). Because of his covenant relationship with Israel, YHWH thwarted all attempts to curse them and turned the cursing into blessing (Num 24:10). This reflects the promise to Abraham in Genesis: "I will bless those who bless you, and the one who curses you I will curse" (Gen 12:3 NRSV).[66] In the book of Ruth it is probably not incidental that the subject of blessing is highlighted, and a woman from the country whose king tried to curse Israel is witness to how YHWH's blessing is a subject on everyone's lips.

Boaz immediately noticed Ruth and inquired about her. His opening question reveals the sort of society that he lived in — he asks not her name but the identity of her owner.[67] This question, "Whose young woman is this?" (ESV), highlights the inferior status of women at that time. As Ellen van Wolde observes: "Ruth is not just an illegal alien in Bethlehem but also a woman, in a society in which women only become someone as 'wife of,' 'daughter of,' 'sister of.' So when all these men — the husband, the father or the brother — disappear, such a woman completely ceases to exist."[68] Ruth's vulnerability as a woman, a stranger, and an unknown person is highlighted. Fewell and Gunn try to imagine how Ruth would have felt when she heard the question about to whom she belonged, and they imagine that she probably inwardly answered the question, "'Whose young woman is this?' . . . Whose, he had said. Whose. Nobody's, she thought. Nobody's hired worker. Nobody's wife. Nobody's mother. Nobody's daughter. Nobody's sister. I suppose that makes me a

---

64. Hubbard comments that the characters need not even be understood as pious at all; what is important is not the piety of the speakers but the presence of the one whose name is voiced (*Ruth,* 144).

65. Ibid., 145.

66. This paragraph, with a few modifications, is taken from my article "Blessing and Curses," 87, and is used with permission.

67. Trible points out that Boaz's question "fits his culture, but does not fit this woman, who is in tension with that culture" (*God and Rhetoric,* 176).

68. Van Wolde, *Ruth and Naomi,* 2.

nobody too."[69] While it is impossible to know what Ruth was thinking, Fewell and Gunn draw attention to the hopeless situation in which Ruth found herself. She was a foreigner, "a nobody." The supervisor informed Boaz that this was the Moabite woman who returned with Naomi. The supervisor showed that he had done his job well: he could identify the woman, explaining who she was and where she had come from. However, he confirmed her feeling of not belonging — of being nobody. He could have said that she was the widow of Mahlon, the son of Elimelech and Naomi, and he could even have described her as Naomi's daughter-in-law. These descriptions would have emphasized that she belonged in Bethlehem. However, the supervisor used the description that highlighted her foreignness. She was the one who came from Moab.

The supervisor's report to Boaz describing what Ruth requested has been the subject of much discussion. He reported to Boaz, "She said, 'Please let me glean and gather among the sheaves after the reapers.' So she came, and she has continued from early morning until now, except for a short rest" (Ruth 2:7 ESV). A significant detail in this report is that Ruth requested permission to gather among the sheaves. The biblical evidence for the practice of gleaning suggests that it took place mainly at the edges and corners of the field (Lev 19:9; 23:22). There is also evidence that the gleaners could gather anything that was dropped or missed by the harvesters in the open field (Lev 19:10; Deut 24:19-21). Only in the book of Ruth is there any mention of gleaning among sheaves. Some scholars argue that Ruth was asking for special privileges that went beyond what was usually permitted; thus her request was bold. But why would she do this? Sasson contends that "Ruth was deliberately presenting the overseer with a request he was not in a position to grant."[70] According to this view, Ruth wanted to meet the owner of the field and therefore asked for something that only he could grant. This assumes that Ruth had not been gleaning before Boaz arrived but had been waiting for him. The second part of the verse has often been cited in support of this approach.

וַתָּבוֹא וַתַּעֲמוֹד מֵאָז הַבֹּקֶר וְעַד־עַתָּה זֶה שִׁבְתָּה הַבַּיִת מְעָט/*wattābô' watta'ămôd mē'āz habbōqer wĕ'ad-'attâ zeh šibtāh habbayit mĕ'āṭ,* "So she came, and she has continued from early morning until now, except for a short rest." (ESV)

The Hebrew word that is translated "and she has continued" (*watta'ămôd*) usually means "and she stood." This has given rise to the interpretation favored by Hubbard and Sasson that she was not given permission by the foreman

---

69. Fewell and Gunn, *Compromising Redemption*, 36.
70. Sasson, *Ruth*, 47.

and had been standing around waiting for Boaz all morning. This approach is supported by the LXX, which reads, "she came and stood from morning till evening and rested not even a little in the field." The Hebrew is not entirely clear, as can be seen from the following literal translation: "She came and she stood from then the morning and until now, this her rest the house a little." The main problem concerns whether the verb "to stand" refers in this context to Ruth standing and waiting or standing and working. Furthermore, what about "the house"? How can there have been a house on the harvest field? We must also identify which noun is qualified by the adjective "little." Is it a "little house" or a "little rest"?

This is obviously a very difficult verse to translate and interpret, and our conclusions must be tentative. However, the argument that Ruth was standing waiting and not working is difficult to support in the light of 2:3, which states that Ruth came to the field and began gleaning immediately: "So she set out and went and gleaned in the field after the reapers, and she happened to come to the part of the field belonging to Boaz, who was of the clan of Elimelech" (ESV). In this verse there is no hint of a period when Ruth was standing around idle. If we assume that Ruth had worked incessantly in the hot sun without food or water, it is understandable that she had become exhausted and was just taking advantage of the shade in the workers' shelter when Boaz arrived. The NJPS reflects this understanding: "She has been on her feet ever since she came this morning. She has rested but little in the hut" (2:7). Perhaps as the owner of the field arrived, everyone made sure that they were working hard. Ruth had been on her feet all morning and needed some shade and respite from the relentless heat of the sun. She was unacquainted with the owner of the field, and anyway she was working for Naomi and herself, not for him. At that time she was unaware of how significant her relationship with this particular boss would become. Therefore at that very moment as Boaz arrived and everyone else was working hard, she went to the workers' hut or shelter for a short rest. Since she did not know anyone in the field, she was alone and obviously a stranger. This had the effect of drawing Boaz's attention, and he asked the supervisor who was this woman who was taking a rest while everyone else was working. This view is supported by Kirsten Nielsen, who suggests that because Ruth was resting when he arrived, "Boaz wonders who she is and what she is doing in his field."[71] The reference that the supervisor made to "gleaning among the sheaves" may have been an attempt on his behalf to get special privileges for Ruth, but this is far from clear.

---

71. Nielsen, *Ruth,* 58.

2:8-13 The First Conversation between Boaz and Ruth

Boaz responded favorably and with generosity. Although a complete stranger, Ruth could not have received a warmer welcome or a more generous offer. His opening words, "Now listen, my daughter" (2:8), are a strong affirmation that she was welcome in his field. These words are phrased as a question in Hebrew, "Have you not heard?" This is a typical way of introducing a strong positive statement in Hebrew (see, e.g., 2 Kgs 19:25).[72]

Although Boaz was meeting her for the first time, he referred to her as "my daughter." Naomi had previously spoken to her in this way (2:2) and would do so again (2:22; 3:1, 16, 18). Boaz also would refer to Ruth again as "daughter" during their encounter at the threshing floor (3:10, 11). By addressing her as "daughter," Boaz was adopting a protective and caring attitude toward her. His main concern was that she should not leave his part of the harvest field to glean elsewhere, and the first instruction that he gave her was that she must not go into another field. This means something entirely different in our culture since we automatically think of fields as areas that are surrounded by fences and that are clearly demarcated. To leave one field and enter another in the context of modern farmland requires a very conscious effort of exiting through a gate and entering the new field through its gate. However, in the context of the book of Ruth, there were no gates and the boundaries would have not have been so clear. Boundaries were usually marked by stones, and there are prohibitions in the OT against moving boundary stones (see, e.g., Deut 19:14; 27:17; Prov 22:28). These would not have prevented Ruth from wandering inadvertently into another person's field. Boaz wanted to treat Ruth well and give her special privileges, but if she wandered into someone else's property, that person could have responded differently. To avoid this happening, Boaz instructed Ruth to "keep close" (ESV, NRSV) to his female workers. These experienced harvesters would provide safety for Ruth and make sure that she did not get into the wrong company. Thus Boaz showed extraordinary concern for someone he had just met.

Apparently Boaz had teams of both female and male harvesters. The text does not differentiate between them in terms of the type of work that they did, but it is clear that they worked in separate teams. The men had the responsibility of keeping the drinking vessels full for the thirsty harvesters. Ruth must stay close to the women, and the men were warned not to touch her. What exactly was Boaz worried about? Apparently a woman on her own, especially a foreigner, needed protection. Boaz's concern highlights the unsavory fact that

---

72. Hubbard, *Ruth*, 154, describes Boaz's opening words to Ruth, which are in the form of a question, as "a typical Hebrew way to express strong affirmations."

although the people living in Bethlehem claimed allegiance to YHWH, there were those who would take advantage of a vulnerable female. On the other hand, Boaz was not simply protecting Ruth. In asking her to stay close to his women, he was also giving her a sense of identity. She would be no longer alone but part of their community. Thus he was giving her something very precious, a sense of security and a sense of significance as part of his team. In his concern to protect Ruth, Boaz compared very favorably with his ancestors, who put their wives in danger. Abraham did this on two occasions by introducing his wife as his sister, and Isaac followed this practice in relation to Rebekah (Gen 12:13; 20:2; 26:7).

The privileges afforded to Ruth, including access to drinking water, were far greater than she had expected. As Bush comments, "Ruth can hardly believe her ears. So stunned and puzzled by such unexpected generosity is she that she falls to the ground in gratitude in the oriental posture of obeisance and asks how it is that she a foreigner should be so favored."[73] Ruth bowed down before Boaz with her face to the ground (Ruth 2:10). This was an act of deep respect and an acknowledgment of her sense of weakness and dependence. She asked, "Why have I found favor in your eyes?" This is a frequently used Hebrew idiom expressing appreciation that is still current in Modern Hebrew. Ruth showed surprise that anyone should take notice of a foreigner like her.

Her short statement showed that she was bewildered by this display of generosity and benevolence. Ruth's attitude was quite different from that of Naomi. Naomi wondered why God could deal so harshly with her, but Ruth wondered why Boaz could deal so generously with her since she was a foreigner — an alien (2:10). Ruth may have expected to attract suspicion and alienation in Bethlehem. Instead Boaz greeted her warmly and accepted her as a person to be welcomed, not as an alien to be kept at a distance and shunned. Ruth was very conscious of her foreign origins, and she revealed this by employing words that sound similar and make this verse, as Campbell suggests, "a pure delight."[74] He is referring particularly to the clause "that you should take notice of me, since I am a foreigner": לְהַכִּירֵנִי וְאָנֹכִי נָכְרִיָּה/*lĕhakkîrēnî wĕʾānōkî nokrîyâ*. The narrator is creating in the reader's mind a favorable impression of Ruth as a hard-working woman who took nothing for granted and appreciated every act of kindness shown to her. She fully understood that she was a foreigner who did not belong in Israel but whose native home was far away. This seems to have been weighing heavily on her mind. It is the burden that exiles must carry, and it is something that a few years' residence will not erase. Rural communities take

73. Bush, "Ruth," 128.
74. Campbell, *Ruth,* 98.

a long time to accept a newcomer. Even in some of the close-knit communities in rural Ireland, someone who has lived in the community for twenty years or more may still be considered an "outsider," and such people are often referred to by the locals as a "blow in"! Israelite communities were also very close-knit, and Ruth the Moabite would always be a foreigner in Bethlehem. Although the position of a stranger could be difficult, the way that Ruth was treated reflects a prominent theme in biblical literature of YHWH's concern for the vulnerable (Lev 19:10; 23:22; Deut 24:19; Ps 72:1-4; Isa 10:1-2). This theme of caring for the stranger is also prominent in the NT (Matt 25:31-46).

Even so, the acceptance of a foreigner raised particular questions in the Jewish community since according to Deut 23:3, "no Ammonite or Moabite may enter the assembly of the LORD" (ESV).To deal with this issue, the Targum has additional material, including a question that Ruth asked Boaz about how she could be accepted in Israel in the light of the prohibition that Moabites are not permitted to enter the congregation of the Lord. Boaz replied that this applied only to males (2:11).[75] These concerns are not reflected in the Hebrew text, which emphasizes how unreservedly this Moabite woman was welcomed in Bethlehem.

Although this was the first time that they had met, Boaz made clear that he had heard a great deal about Ruth, including information about the commendable way that she had cared for her mother-in-law after her husband Mahlon had died (Ruth 2:11-12). How could Boaz have heard this information? The only person who could have shared this information was Naomi herself. Naomi had shared her bitter experiences with others, and the news had spread throughout Bethlehem. However, in spite of her sorrow and sadness, Naomi had also shared news about how good Ruth had been. This did not change Ruth's status as a "foreigner," but it did lead to people regarding her favorably. Boaz was particularly impressed that she had left her birthplace and her father's house in order to stay with Naomi and care for her. This is the only mention of Ruth's father in the book and provides a clue that both her father and mother were still alive. It is not surprising that Boaz should think that way. Israel's story began with a man leaving home (Gen 12:1-3). Like Ruth, Abraham had lived as a stranger but had enjoyed the blessing of God. Ruth was probably unaware that she was following in the footsteps of the great patriarch. She did not have promises of blessing to rely on. Thus the treatment she received was a very welcome surprise.[76]

---

75. Levine, *Aramaic Version of Ruth*, 26.

76. Robert Alter argues that there is a clear allusion in the words of Boaz to the call of Abraham. He refers to the "identical verbal cluster, land-birthplace-father," which occurs in the call of Abraham and in Boaz's reference to Ruth's commitment (*World of Biblical Literature*, 51).

Boaz expressed the wish or prayer that Ruth would be rewarded for her deeds and repaid in full. By saying the same thing in two different ways he emphasized that Ruth deserved to be repaid for her faithfulness and good deeds. As Gow observes, the passage emphasizes that "Ruth's loyalty to her mother-in-law merits the blessing of the God of Israel."[77]

Boaz also suggested that he had heard something about Ruth's faith. He mentioned that she had come to seek refuge under the "wings" of the God of Israel (2:12). Wings were a suggestive metaphor in Israel, signifying strength and protection. They are mentioned in connection with the exodus of Israel from Egypt when God's role is described as carrying his people out of Egypt on eagles' wings (Exod 19:4). In the Psalms God's wings or the shadow of his wings provide protection for those who seek refuge in him (Pss 17:8; 36:7; 57:1; 61:4; 91:4). The word "wing" was also used to denote the corner of a garment, and it occurs in this context later in the story (Ruth 3:9; cf. Num 15:38; Ezek 5:3; Zech 8:23). As Paul House points out, "Boaz's personal theology may be summarized in this blessing. He believes that God does reward all who take shelter in the Lord."[78] Receiving shelter means to be protected, and Boaz believed that by coming to Israel, Ruth had placed herself under God's protection. This role of God as "protector" is also prominent in Genesis. Before sending the flood God provided a means of protection for Noah and his family and also for the animals and birds (Gen 6:17-20). When Abraham endangered his wife in Egypt and later in the Philistine territory, God protected Sarah and saved her from the clutches of both Pharaoh and Abimelech (Gen 12:17; 20:3-7). In his appearance to Abraham in Genesis 15, YHWH described himself as "your shield, your very great reward" (Gen 15:1 NIV). Furthermore, in the account of Jacob the theme of protection is particularly prominent. God protected him not only from Esau and Laban but also from the inhabitants of Canaan following the slaughter of the Shechemites (Gen 28–35). Whether Ruth had personal faith in YHWH as her protector is not clear.

Boaz expressed the wish that Ruth would receive a "full reward" from YHWH in recognition of all that she had done (Ruth 2:12). The word translated "reward," מַשְׂכֹּרֶת/*maśkōret*, is used in the story of Jacob and Laban, where it is usually translated "wages" (Gen 29:15; 31:7, 41). It refers to something that is deserved, and Boaz believed that, unlike Laban, God would repay Ruth generously.[79] Perhaps this is a reflection of Boaz's own experience of God's generosity

---

77. Gow, *Book of Ruth*, 104.

78. Paul R. House, *Old Testament Theology*, 459.

79. Hubbard helpfully compares the story of Laban's miserly approach to Jacob with the generous way that Boaz believed Ruth would be rewarded because her "paymaster" was "Yahweh the God of Israel" (*Ruth*, 167).

in blessing the people of Bethlehem with an abundant harvest after the time of famine.

Ruth responded to Boaz with gratitude and humility. Her response gives us an insight into how she had been feeling. She probably somewhat nervously expressed the desire that she will continue to "find favor" in Boaz's eyes (Ruth 2:13 NIV). In other words, she was delighted that he had been pleased with what he had heard about her and she hoped that she would continue to be pleasing in his sight. This is an acknowledgment that she still felt very vulnerable and that she was fully aware that she would continue to need help in the future. The second aspect of her response was her gratitude because Boaz had comforted her (*pi'el* of נחם/*nḥm*). The verb, especially in the *pi'el,* is often used in the context of comforting the bereaved (e.g., Gen 37:35; 2 Sam 12:24; Isa 61:2; Jer 16:7). Ruth's departure from Moab after her husband's death would have left her with a deep sense of bereavement and vulnerability, but now this overwhelming generosity from a complete stranger had brought comfort and security. Ruth continued her expression of gratitude by remarking that Boaz had spoken "kindly" to her. Literally the Hebrew idiom that she used is, "you have spoken upon the heart." This idiom is used elsewhere in the OT with slightly different nuances of meaning (see, e.g., Gen 34:3; 50:21; Judg 19:3; 2 Sam 19:7; 2 Chr 30:22; Isa 40:2; Hos 2:16). In these occurrences the person who speaks "upon the heart" is usually either developing a good relationship with the subject (Gen 34:3) or bringing necessary comfort and encouragement (2 Chr 30:22; Isa 40:2). Both these motives were present in Boaz's speech. He was encouraging and comforting Ruth since she had endured much hardship, and at the same time he was in the early stages of developing a relationship of trust with her.

Ruth finished her response by acknowledging that she was not even as high in status as one of his servant women and yet Boaz had treated her so well (Ruth 2:13). What had happened to her was greater than someone at her low status could have expected. As Hubbard suggests, "her words sounded like a great, joyous sigh of relief after the days of uncertainty since her husband's death."[80]

2:14-17 Boaz's Generosity

Boaz invited Ruth to eat along with the reapers, and his generosity is expressed by the observation that she had enough food to satisfy her and she also had some left over. This pattern is evident in other biblical stories about the provision of food. The provider of a meal knows that his guest has had enough

80. Ibid., 171.

when those dining have some left over. This is mentioned specifically when Elisha fed a hundred men with twenty loaves (2 Kgs 4:44) and when Jesus fed five thousand with five loaves (John 6:12-13). In both cases the amount left over was significant because it showed that the supply of food had been abundant. It also showed that people really had sufficient food to satisfy them and that they were not simply being polite and refraining from eating to leave enough for others. In the story of Ruth the leftover food not only shows that she had more than enough to eat, but also highlights her thoughtfulness since she kept the surplus food in order to give it to Naomi later (Ruth 2:18).

Following the meal, Boaz continued to act on Ruth's behalf. His kind words to her were translated into action. He commanded his men to allow her to glean even among the sheaves themselves, and he made clear that they were not to embarrass her. Furthermore they were instructed to encourage her by pulling out some grain deliberately and leaving it for her. This is what is meant by the quaint KJV rendering, "handfuls of purpose." Boaz's generosity was exemplary and provided a lifeline to the foreign widow and her mother-in-law.

Ruth now felt secure and under Boaz's protection. She worked without fear until evening and gathered enough grain to provide an ephah of barley. It is not quite clear how much this would have weighed. The largest OT measure was a homer, which was equivalent to one donkey load. An ephah was one-tenth of a homer and probably weighed at least twenty-eight pounds. Most scholars agree that this was a massive amount to gather in one day.[81] Hubbard suggests that Ruth's achievement was "truly astonishing," and he comments, "Such a startling quantity of grain testified both to Boaz's generosity and to Ruth's industry."[82]

2:18-23 Ruth's Return to Naomi

Naomi, we may imagine, was waiting anxiously throughout the day for Ruth's return. We can only begin to appreciate the sense of insecurity that she felt in facing an unknown future of hunger and despair. This foreboding that she must have felt helps to highlight and accentuate the wonderful surprise she received when her daughter-in-law returned in the evening with a very impressive amount of barley and the roasted grain that was left from her earlier meal. Imagine the old woman's delight to receive not only an abundant supply of grain but also a prepared meal. This bounty that unexpectedly came her way

---

81. Hubbard suggests that "Ruth collected the equivalent of at least half a month's wages in one day" (ibid., 179).

82. Ibid.

led Naomi to inquire about where Ruth had been gleaning to gather such a large amount of grain, and she uttered a blessing on the person concerned even though, at that stage, she did not know his identity (Ruth 2:19).

Ruth revealed that the man's name was Boaz. Ruth did not know the relationship of Boaz to Elimelech and Naomi. Bush comments on the "delightful irony" in the story since the reader knows more than the characters.[83] Ruth knew that she had been with Boaz, and this is something that Naomi did not know. On the other hand, Ruth did not realize that Naomi knew that Boaz was a relative. However, Naomi soon enlightened Ruth, because when she heard that the person concerned was Boaz, she exclaimed, "May he be blessed by the LORD" ESV (2:20). Perhaps this was just a simple exclamation of surprise or joy meaning no more than, "Well done, Boaz!" On the other hand, blessing was taken very seriously in biblical narratives, and the invocation of blessing may be much more than simply an exclamation of surprise. When God bestowed blessing, it meant that he gave the person success. We must not allow our modern usage of this term to blind us to its significance and importance in the ancient world. It is a major theme in Genesis, where a father's blessing was important enough to create family strife and envy and led even to the threat of murder (Gen 27:41). Blessing was more than just a good wish but rather implied the giving of power to succeed. Naomi recognized that such generosity as Boaz had shown deserved recognition, and it was her desire that the Lord should bless such a generous person, or, in other words, that God should give him good success and repay him for his generosity to Ruth.

However, to understand Naomi's response in relation to Boaz we need to decide to whom she is referring when she states that he has not "not stopped showing his kindness" (Ruth 2:20 NIV). The Hebrew is ambiguous: this could refer to Boaz or to YHWH. Some scholars maintain that it is Boaz who has not stopped showing his kindness.[84] Bush argues very strongly for this view and concludes that "it seems unquestionable that Boaz is the antecedent of the relative clause."[85]

In order to resolve this issue, we need to establish whether Naomi's exclamation relates to the large amount of grain or to the surprising fact that Ruth had met such a prominent person. If she was referring to the grain, then it is Boaz whose kindness had not forsaken them; but if she was referring to the good news that Ruth has met Boaz, then this is a recognition that YHWH was at work behind the scenes on her behalf. Naomi had already highlighted

83. Bush, "Ruth," 141.
84. Gow, *Book of Ruth*, 60, 105.
85. Bush, "Ruth," 136.

the generosity of the person who gave so much to Ruth, and this further exclamation was related to the remarkable news that Ruth had met Boaz. Does
she give praise to God for this meeting or to Boaz? This timely meeting with
one of the people that could help them was not planned by Naomi but it was
great news. Boaz had not planned the meeting either, and so to say that he had
"not stopped showing his kindness" simply because he gave Ruth grain seems
to miss the point. Furthermore, her reference was to the one "whose kindness
has not forsaken the living or the dead" (2:20 ESV). Boaz was certainly showing kindness to the living, but it is difficult to see how he has shown kindness
to the dead by giving grain to Ruth. Therefore, she was probably referring to
YHWH, not to Boaz. Boaz had not been in touch with the family for over ten
years, and the narrator has not given us an indication of what the relationship
was like prior to that time. Boaz's acts of kindness are not under discussion, but
YHWH's faithfulness was certainly an important issue for Naomi.

Feeling forsaken by God is one of the main themes of the book. Naomi
had accused Shaddai of dealing bitterly with her, and she had accused YHWH
of making life difficult for her. Now with the news of the "providential accident"
— the contact with Boaz — she realized that in spite of all that had happened,
YHWH, whom her husband and she had trusted many years previously, had
not forsaken her after all and was still showing faithfulness to her and to her
family. This unplanned meeting was a sign to Naomi that God was in control
of the situation and had not forgotten about them. The Hebrew word translated
"kindness" (חֶסֶד/ḥesed) carries rich and profound theological meaning that is
not adequately conveyed in the English translation. The Hebrew term is used
in contexts where not only the concept of kindness is present, but also the idea
of faithfulness and steadfast love (cf. Hos 6:6). "Faithful love" would be a good
translation.

Naomi's faith had been challenged, and when she returned to Bethlehem
she freely admitted that she had been disappointed with God. Now, however,
the flame of faith was rekindled as she became aware that far from forsaking
her, God was at work and was providing for her, albeit through her foreign
daughter-in-law whom she had tried to leave behind in Moab. These are the
most positive words that Naomi had spoken so far, and this may be understood
as a turning point in the book.[86] The enormous pile of grain had reassured her
that someone had been kind to Ruth, but when she heard that Ruth had met her
relative Boaz, this was indeed too wonderful to be simply a coincidence, and

---

86. Sakenfeld suggests that the response from Naomi to Ruth's declaration that she has
been in Boaz's field "may be regarded as the turning point of the story both theologically and
rhetorically" (*Ruth*, 47).

with great relief she realized that God had not forgotten about them and was working on their behalf. Thus the bitter Naomi became the positive, praising Naomi because now there was hope. Naomi was now convinced that YHWH was working on their behalf because he had led Ruth to one of the people who could help them.

Naomi's joyful outburst had prevented Ruth from saying everything that was on her heart, and now she had an opportunity to finish her story. She was eager to tell Naomi everything, but her version of the story was not entirely accurate. Ruth changed what Boaz told her to suit her own desires and aspirations. Clearly Boaz had told her to "keep close to my young women" (2:8 ESV); but in reporting this advice, Ruth declared that Boaz told her to "keep close by my young men" (2:21 ESV; cf. KJV). LaCocque suggests that this was a mistake on Ruth's part brought about by her different cultural background. He argues that women were more liberated in Moab than in Judah, and Ruth's suggestion that she would stay with the male servants would have been acceptable in Moab but not Judah.[87] However, perhaps Ruth's deliberate misquoting of Boaz has a more significant meaning. Ruth recognized her need of a partner, and staying close to young women was certainly not going to improve her chance of marriage. It was not a cultural faux pas that lay behind her desire to stay with the men, but a feeling of desperation and insecurity about the future. Ruth had already shown that she could take the initiative, and her pressing need for a husband was in danger of clouding her judgment. Perhaps this is why she told Naomi that Boaz had told her to stay close to the young men. Naomi apparently saw immediately that this was very unlikely, and she advised her daughter-in-law to "go out with his young women" (2:22 ESV). Ruth could not see at this stage that the God of Israel was in control of her destiny, and who can blame her for wanting to associate with the young men of Bethlehem, among whom she could possibly find the husband who would provide the security she and Naomi so much needed. This insight that the narrator gives us to Ruth's inner sense of insecurity and impatience adds tension to the story and enables the reader to empathize with this vulnerable Moabite and to understand the tension and insecurity that she struggled with.

The need to wait for YHWH's plan to unfold is thus one of the themes of this book. It would be a tragedy if Ruth married the wrong person because of impatience. Even Abraham and Sarah had shown impatience, and Abraham had married Hagar with disastrous consequences (Gen 16:1-16). Ruth, however, unlike Abraham and Sarah, showed remarkable patience; and although the advice given by both Boaz and Naomi may have not been exactly what she wanted,

---

87. LaCocque, *Ruth,* 78-79.

she accepted that they knew what was best for her and obeyed their instruction: "she kept close to the young women of Boaz" (Ruth 2:23 ESV). Thus the narrator gradually builds a very favorable profile of Ruth through showing her respect for Naomi and her willingness to follow the older person's instructions in spite of her own desires. Later in the story, Boaz would acknowledge and praise Ruth's patience in that she had not "run after the younger men, whether rich or poor" (3:10 NIV).

Naomi's outburst of praise and gratitude needed an explanation. Why had she suddenly turned from despair to hope? She explained to Ruth that this person into whose field she had stumbled, as if by accident, was a family member and one of their "redeemers," which meant that he had the right to redeem her dead husband's property (2:20). Elimelech had not sold his land before leaving for Moab.[88] It would have been very difficult to do so during a famine. Furthermore, there were traditions and laws governing landownership. Land that had been sold when a family faced hard times could be bought back again so that it remained within the family. If someone could not afford to buy back their land, their next of kin could do this for them; this person was known as a "redeemer" (Lev 25:23-31).[89] Naomi realized that Boaz was a man who could fulfill this responsibility. This is why Naomi believed that YHWH was showing his faithful love not only to the living but also to the dead. The understanding of landownership meant that the memory of her dead husband was involved in this question of land inheritance. However, although Boaz was the ideal person to turn her family tragedy into future blessing and prosperity, Naomi did not know if he was willing to act on their behalf. Thus there remains tension and uncertainty in the story, especially since Boaz was not the only one who had the right to redeem the land. Thus she described him as "one of our redeemers" (Ruth 2:20 ESV)

Chapter 2 concludes with a brief summary of the situation, confirming that Ruth kept close to the young women of Boaz, gleaning until the end of the barley and wheat harvests (2:23), a period of about seven weeks (Deut 16:9). Thus the immediate needs of Naomi and Ruth had been taken care of. The final statement of v. 23 (ESV) indicates that Ruth "lived with her mother-in-law." Ruth therefore spent her time in two places: during the day in the fields of Boaz, and in the evening and at night in her mother-in-law's home.

88. This point is made clear later in the book when Boaz revealed that Naomi had land to sell that once belonged to her husband, Elimelech (Ruth 4:3).

89. This tradition of maintaining family ownership of land is reflected in the story of Naboth (1 Kgs 21). In the reign of King Ahab, Naboth refused to sell his land to the king because it belonged to his family. Even the king could not force a man to sell his family's land. Ahab and Jezebel had to resort to corrupt practice: Naboth was falsely accused, executed, and his land confiscated.

3:1-5 Naomi's Plan

Ruth had taken the initiative to go and glean in one of the fields, and this had worked out better than she or Naomi could have imagined. This arrangement provided the food that she and Naomi required during harvest, but Naomi recognized the need for a long-term solution. This time it was not Ruth who took the initiative but Naomi. Boaz had made no move to purchase the land. Was Naomi disappointed? She had been excited and thrilled when Boaz showed an interest in Ruth; but since then the days and weeks had passed by and there was no sign of Boaz showing a deeper interest in her or Ruth, and there was no indication that he was interested in the land. The time had come for Naomi to act, even though there were serious risks involved. She was a resourceful woman who realized that nothing was going to happen without her intervention. It was one of those situations where faith and action went hand in hand.

She asked Ruth, "My daughter, should I not seek rest for you, that it may be well with you?" (Ruth 3:1 ESV). What did Naomi mean by "seek rest"? This word for "rest" is used in Lam 1:3 indicating that the people of Judah in exile have no resting place (see also Deut 28:65). The same word is also used in the flood narrative. The dove returned to the ark because there was no "resting place" (Gen 8:9). In this context the reference is to Ruth's status as a widow in a strange land. The desired "resting place" is a secure home with a husband to care for her. There is an obvious reference back to Naomi's words to Orpah and Ruth in the land of Moab, "The LORD grant that you may find rest, each of you in the house of her husband!" (Ruth 1:9 ESV).

Naomi knew that the harvest time was coming to an end. Boaz was winnowing the grain that had been harvested. Time was limited, and Boaz had not made his intentions known. Naomi decided to test him. The plan was a daring one and included an element of risk. Phyllis Trible describes Naomi's plan as "an outrageous scheme, dangerous and delicate."[90] Block comments, "Ruth's preparations and the choice of location for the encounter suggest the actions of a prostitute."[91] Furthermore, Moabites had a reputation for seducing Israelites (Num 25:1-2).

Naomi explained her plan to Ruth with careful attention to detail. She advised Ruth to go to the harvest field and to watch Boaz carefully as he ate and drank and then prepared to retire for the night. The reference to eating and drinking is significant since a meal was an appropriate setting and context for receiving a blessing. In Genesis the blessing bestowed by Isaac did not proceed

90. Trible, *God and Rhetoric*, 182.
91. Block, "Ruth," 609.

until a hearty meal of his favorite food was provided. Blessings were bestowed on someone in a harmonious relationship with the donor. Thus, in the Genesis story, the meal that both sons prepared was intended to make sure that Isaac was in the right frame of mind to bestow the blessing (Gen 27:1-29). Likewise in this story, Naomi wanted Ruth to approach Boaz at an appropriate time when he was in the right frame of mind to fulfill her request (Ruth 3:1-3).

Naomi instructed Ruth to wash, wear her best clothes, and use perfume. Some think that the instructions that Naomi gives Ruth suggest that she was to dress and prepare herself like a bride for a wedding. However, Bush makes the interesting suggestion that Naomi was instructing Ruth to lay aside her widow's clothes, thereby bringing to an end the outward signs of mourning for her dead husband, and "so signal her return to the normal activities and desires of life, which, of course, would include marriage."[92] If Ruth has been wearing clothes associated with mourning up until this point, Boaz would now see her in an entirely new light.

Once she reached the harvest field Ruth was instructed to watch Boaz from a distance but not to let him see her. The element of surprise was crucial. She must watch carefully where he lay down, since she must be sure that she was approaching the right person in the darkness; what a scandal it would be if she approached the wrong man! Then Ruth was instructed to uncover Boaz's feet and to lie down there. Commentators have struggled somewhat with this particular instruction. Hubbard suggests that the reason for uncovering the feet of Boaz was so that the cold air would cause him to awaken so that Ruth would have an opportunity to speak to him.[93] However, Tod Linafelt rejects this suggestion and argues that such speculation is "simply unjustified by the story."[94]

Ruth did not question Naomi's instructions but followed them obediently (3:5). We can speculate that Naomi's purpose in proposing this risky strategy was to find an opportunity for Ruth to meet Boaz alone. Ruth's lowly status did not allow her simply to accost Boaz during daylight and begin a conversation with him. Naomi also realized that Boaz would be reluctant to pay too much attention to Ruth in full view of his workers. He would not want gossip about his relationship to Ruth to spread throughout Bethlehem. This is why Naomi contrived this plan to allow Ruth to meet Boaz alone and in secret. It was risky, since if anyone saw them the suggestion of inappropriate behavior would ruin both their reputations.

---

92. Bush, "Ruth," 152.

93. Hubbard, *Ruth,* 204. Hubbard suggests that "Naomi cleverly figured that he would not awaken until aware of the discomfort."

94. Tod Linafelt, "Ruth," 53.

3:6-9 The Visit at Midnight

Ruth carried out her mother-in-law's instructions to the letter. She observed Boaz eating and drinking before he lay down beside his pile of grain. This practice was common; unprotected grain was vulnerable to theft and also to animals or birds rummaging for food. However, Sasson contends that there must be another reason for Boaz's activity: "Boaz was far too important a man to keep watch through the night; he most certainly could have asked one of his many 'men' to assume such a charge. Additionally, it would certainly have been strange for any man to prepare for an all-night vigil by copiously consuming food and drink."[95] LaCocque points out that the Midrash "finds a nobler reason" for Boaz sleeping on the threshing floor — he wanted to avoid it being used for immoral purposes.[96]

During the night (lit. "at midnight") Boaz was startled to discover a woman lying at his feet on the threshing floor. He was probably alarmed at first. He obviously could not recognize the woman in the darkness and asked, "Who are you?" However, he did know that it was a woman since he used the feminine pronoun in his question. Ruth, the widowed Moabite daughter-in-law of Naomi, identified herself simply as "Ruth, your servant" (3:9).

Having identified herself, Ruth asked him to spread his garment over her. She used the Hebrew word for "wing," but this is used frequently to refer to the wing or corner of a garment (e.g., 1 Sam 15:27). However, it also recalls Boaz's reference to sheltering under God's wings (Ruth 2:12). Thus far Ruth had followed Naomi's instructions to the letter; but now, for the first time, she went beyond what Naomi had told her to do by reminding Boaz of his status as a "redeemer" (גֹּאֵל/gōʾēl). The gōʾēl was usually associated with buying property back for a family that had fallen on hard times (Lev 25:23-28). On the one hand, Ruth's appearance at the threshing floor, her dress and perfume, made this virtually a proposal of marriage; but on the other hand, her mention of the gōʾēl also included the purchase of the land of Elimelech and the provision of security for Naomi. In raising the issue of the land, Ruth took the initiative and went beyond what Naomi told her to do. Both Naomi and Ruth showed admirable qualities since they were concerned about each other. Naomi's concern was primarily for Ruth, and her plan for the meeting at the threshing floor did not include the "redemption" of the land. However, Ruth was not so absorbed by her own aspirations as to forget the one she pledged never to leave or forsake.

95. Sasson, *Ruth,* 65.
96. LaCocque, *Ruth,* 94. See Rabinowitz, *Midrash Rabbah: Ruth,* V.15 (p. 72).

3:10-15 Boaz's Response to Ruth's Plea

Boaz's response was warm and spiritual: "May you be blessed by the LORD, my daughter" (Ruth 3:10 ESV). Boaz was delighted that Ruth had come to him, and he expressed gratitude that she had not "gone after young men, whether poor or rich" (3:10 ESV). We are not told why Boaz is relieved that Ruth had not found a young husband. Perhaps this suggests that he wanted to marry her but had not wanted to pressure her; at the same time he was concerned that she would find someone else. Now he was pleased that she had come to him. Boaz praised her for her conduct. Most versions translate חֶסֶד/*ḥesed* by "kindness," but the NRSV has "loyalty," which conveys the meaning much better. "Kindness" is misleading in this context. She needed kindness from others, but what she showed was grit and commitment in not giving up hope and in making the bold and difficult visit to the threshing floor. Boaz states that her second deed of loyalty was greater than the first. What was he referring to? Her first deed of loyalty was to accompany her mother-in-law to Bethlehem. Her second deed of loyalty was to approach him not just as a marriage partner but as a *gōʾēl* who could also provide security for Naomi. Her first priority was always Naomi. She had shown loyalty and had waited for the right time as guided by her mother-in-law. Boaz must have noticed that she was very nervous; perhaps her voice gave her away. He sought to reassure her and calm her fears. "And now, my daughter, do not fear. I will do for you all that you ask" (3:11 ESV). Since she had not asked for anything specifically, it is clear that the approach that Naomi had choreographed was understood in their culture as a way of making a request for marriage. Ruth's personal initiative in reminding Boaz that he was their *gōʾēl* made perfectly clear what she wanted him to do. She not only wanted security for herself but also for Naomi.

Then Boaz uses a strange expression: "all the gate of my people know that you are a woman of strength" (3:11, my trans.). The word "gate" has been translated in a number of ways. One may argue that it should be translated as "city," since all the people in the city must go through the "gate" (KJV). Most modern translations understand the term to relate to the townsfolk in general or to all the men of the town (e.g., NKJV, NLT, ESV, NIV). However, these translations do not explain why the people of the city should be described as "the gate." The "gate" was the center where people assembled and where judgments were made. On this basis preferable translations are "all the assembly of my people" (NRSV) or "all the elders of my town" (NJPS). Thus Boaz assures Ruth that she is highly regarded, especially by those in authority. He explains that she is regarded as אֵשֶׁת חַיִל/*ʾēšet ḥayil* (3:11). This term is translated in various ways: "you are a worthy woman" (ESV); "you are a woman of noble character" (NIV); "you are a virtuous woman" (NKJV). However, the word *ḥayil* is usually translated "valor" or "strength"; it is one of the adjectives employed earlier to describe Boaz as a "worthy man" (2:1 ESV). It is used of the virtuous wife in Proverbs 31. In spite of the hardship she had faced and the disadvantages associated with being "foreign," Ruth had proved to be a woman of character and resolve. Her exemplary behavior had won her a good reputation among the most influential people in Bethlehem.

LaCocque makes the interesting comment that from 3:12 "the language becomes rocky" as Boaz uses up to five "useless words." LaCocque suggests that Boaz may have been "stammering in his confusion" or "searching for words."[97] Boaz's hesitation introduces tension into the narrative. Boaz was very supportive and willing to help, but there was a complication. Although Boaz was a *gō'ēl*, "kinsman" or "redeemer," there was another, closer relative who had to be permitted to exercise his rights if he wished. Only if he refused could Boaz become involved. Perhaps this is why Boaz had not already suggested redeeming the family property — he realized that he did not have this right since someone else had a prior claim on the property. Boaz did not want complications to arise later, and he resolved to clarify the issues at this stage.

Boaz invited Ruth to stay on the threshing floor until the morning. There is a careful choice of words. Boaz could have invited her "to lie down" or "to sleep" there until morning. But the verbs "to lie" and "to sleep" can refer to sexual relations. However, Boaz invites her "to lodge," which, although an unusual verb to use in this context, removes any ambiguity and makes clear that he has no hidden agenda. His relationship with Ruth will not become closer until he has sorted out the legal problems. As Michael Goulder wittily suggests, what happened at the threshing floor was all highly symbolical and not at all immoral: "The idea is taken to be sheerly symbolic; no hanky-panky is implied and the whole atmosphere is pure as the driven snow."[98]

Boaz sent Ruth back to Naomi before daylight. He did not want to start a scandal. He provided Ruth with six "measures" of grain to take to Naomi. Since the size of the measure is not given, there has been considerable speculation. It is generally agreed that the "measure" could not refer to an ephah since six ephahs would be over five hundred pounds, and thus too heavy for Ruth to carry. According to the Targum, the measure was a seah, which is one-third of an ephah. The Targum explains that Ruth was given "strength and power from before the Lord" to enable her to carry such a heavy load (3:15).[99] Another

---

97. LaCocque, *Ruth*, 100.
98. Michael D. Goulder, "Ruth: A Homily on Deuteronomy 22–25?" 317.
99. Levine, *Aramaic Version of Ruth*, 95.

possibility is that the measure in this context is an omer, which is one-tenth of an ephah. This would have weighed about fifty pounds and was less than Ruth had gleaned during her first day in Boaz's field (Ruth 2:17). Nevertheless, this would have been a substantial load to carry, especially early in the morning. At any rate, since Boaz has to help Ruth to lift the grain, a considerable amount is implied, and the emphasis is on his generosity.

3:16-18 Ruth Returns to Naomi

When Ruth returned to her mother-in-law, according to the Hebrew text, Naomi asks, "Who are you, my daughter?" (3:16). This is a very strange question for Naomi to ask Ruth, and most modern versions avoid translating it literally and assume that Naomi was asking, "How did you fare?" (ESV) or "How did it go?" (NIV). However, if we try to make sense of the Hebrew as it stands, it may mean that Naomi was actually asking, "Who are you now?" In any case Naomi is echoing the very words used by Boaz on the threshing floor. Naomi was perhaps inquiring about whether Ruth's identity had changed. Had the encounter at the threshing floor given Ruth, the foreign widow, a new identity?

Ruth explained what had happened and showed Naomi the six measures of barley that she received from Boaz. Ruth introduced new information at this point. When the grain was given to her on the threshing floor, we are not told what Boaz actually said. Now Ruth supplied this information and informed Naomi that Boaz's concern was not just for her but also for her mother-in-law. Boaz did not want her to return to her mother-in-law empty-handed. His generosity extended not just to Ruth but also to Naomi herself. Naomi complained that she had come home "empty," but now Boaz had taken responsibility to provide for her.

Now the two of them must wait for the outcome of discussions between Boaz and the other potential redeemer. Waiting would not be easy, but Naomi assured Ruth that Boaz would deal with this matter promptly (3:18). This showed that Naomi had a great deal of respect for Boaz and suggests that she knew he was a man who would not waste any time in carrying out his plan.

4:1-4 The Meeting of Two Redeemers

Boaz met the potential redeemer at the gate of the town. Some ancient towns had both inner and outer gates, the outer for defense and the inner an open space where people could meet and do business. A good example may be seen at

Tel Dan, where Avraham Biran, the archaeologist of the site, has reconstructed the gate to show how it may have been used. The reconstruction includes benches where people could sit and a covered seat for the governor or king.[100]

Boaz summoned the man to a meeting and invited ten elders as witnesses (4:1-2). In later Judaism the number ten would become very significant as the number of men required for a minyan, which is the quorum needed for a public service.[101] Boaz announced that the purpose of the meeting was to discuss the sale of the land that belonged to their relative. A quaint Hebrew idiom is employed by Boaz to introduce the subject. The English translation, "I thought I would tell you of it" (ESV), hides the underlying Hebrew idiom, "I decided to uncover your ear" (4:4).

Boaz made clear that he needed to know whether this close relative of Elimelech was willing to act as redeemer of the property of Elimelech. This transaction would keep the land in the family and give Naomi enough money to live independently. Boaz takes up his position, and when the man appears, Boaz calls him over. The man remains anonymous, but he is referred to in the text as פְּלֹנִי אַלְמֹנִי/*pĕlōnî 'almōnî,* which is usually translated "friend" (ESV, NRSV, NLT) or "my friend" (NIV). The same phrase is also used to refer to "a certain place" or "such and such a place" in two passages, where the actual location must not be revealed (1 Sam 21:2; 2 Kgs 6:8). Clearly, it is used to indicate uncertainty or to avoid using a name. Thus the man's identity is not revealed. There is no doubt that Boaz knew his name and used it in the transaction. Therefore, the anonymity is probably significant in the story and provides a contrast between Boaz and Mr. So-and-So (so NJPS), who lacked the vision, commitment, and compassion of Boaz. Whereas Boaz's name became well known, the other potential redeemer remained anonymous. This may not seem important to us, but it is an important theme for the narrator, who could have told the story perfectly coherently without introducing this phrase *pĕlōnî 'almōnî.* The importance of a great name is a particularly significant theme in Genesis, Ruth, and 1 Samuel. In Genesis the builders of the tower of Babel wanted to make a name for themselves (Gen 11:4). They were not able to achieve this, but in the following chapter God promised Abraham that he would make his name great (12:2). Apart from Abraham, the only other person in the OT who is said to have a "great name" is King David. Moreover, after So-and-So walked away, a blessing was pronounced on Boaz that means, "may you call a name in Bethlehem" (Ruth 4:11). Thus a contrast is made between Boaz and the man who remained So-and-So.

---

100. See Avraham Biran, "Tel Dan," esp. 329 and the picture of the covered seat on 330.
101. I remember being asked on a flight to Israel whether I was Jewish. Apparently the objective was to find ten men (a minyan) to meet to pray at the back of the aircraft.

Before mentioning Ruth, Boaz informed So-and-So about the land that belonged to Naomi. This is new information for the reader. Until now there has been no indication that Naomi had land for sale, and the reader will have assumed that she was destitute and dependent on charity. This raises many questions about how a widow could actually inherit land and about why the narrator is silent about it until now. It suggests that when Elimelech left Bethlehem, he did not sell the land, either because it was impossible to do so during the famine, or because the price that he would have received would have been extremely low. Naomi's claim was that she had gone away full and had come back empty. This indicates that she had to return to Bethlehem because it was the only place where she had anything. There is no indication that the land had been harvested by someone else, and one possibility is that it was lying fallow. It may have been illegal to simply put the land on the open market, and Naomi had to find someone who was Elimelech's next of kin to purchase it. During the harvest there would have been little interest in purchasing land that had not been cultivated, and therefore she had to wait until a good opportunity arose. Apparently the land could be sold only to a family/clan member (cf. Lev 25:23-28), and Naomi may have been waiting to see how the relationship between Boaz and Ruth developed, since the ideal situation was an arrangement that took care of both the land and Ruth at the same time.

According to some English versions, Boaz declares that Naomi "is selling" the land that belonged to Elimelech (ESV, NIV). However, the Hebrew uses the perfect tense of the verb "to sell," and literally it reads, "she has sold." As Bush points out, we cannot take this verb "in its most obvious meaning (as a past tense) and suppose that Naomi 'sold' the field some time in the past."[102] This cannot mean that she has sold it and received the money since they have been depending on charity to survive. Nor could it mean that she sold it while in Moab, since she claimed to have returned empty. Therefore, the idea that she has "sold" the land must be open to another interpretation, since Boaz's intention is to "redeem" the land by buying it from Naomi. The perfect of the verb probably represents the idea that the decision to sell is final. The land has been put up for sale and there is no turning back on that decision. To sell is Naomi's only hope for the future, and therefore the decision to sell is irrevocable. The next stage is to find someone within the family circle to buy (redeem) it.

Boaz explained in the presence of the witnesses that he is willing to redeem the land, but So-and-So was a closer relative than he and must refuse the opportunity to redeem the land before Boaz can exercise his right to buy it. The man's response is immediate and positive — he will buy the land. Land

---

102. Bush, "Ruth," 211.

was difficult to obtain since it was not traded in the open market but was kept within the family.[103] Now that the famine had passed, any opportunity to obtain new land would be welcome.

4:5-6 Boaz Speaks about Ruth

However, before this deal is confirmed, Boaz introduced information that caused the man to change his mind. What exactly was this information? This is a matter of considerable debate, since the Hebrew Bible provides two possible readings for v. 5. Most English versions follow the tradition that Boaz informed So-and-So that if he redeemed the land, he must marry Ruth. The NIV is typical: "Then Boaz said, 'On the day you buy the land from Naomi and from Ruth the Moabitess, you acquire the dead man's widow, in order to maintain the name of the dead with his property.'" The controversy involves the verb קָנִיתָה/*qānîtâ*, which the NIV translates "you acquire." This is the reading in the margin of the Hebrew Bible (Qere), but the consonantal text (Ketib) is קניתי/*qnyty,* which could be translated "I acquire." Thus it is unclear whether Boaz said, "you must marry Ruth" or "I (have decided to) marry Ruth." If we accept the consonantal text, as some scholars do (Beattie, Sasson, Holmstedt, Nielsen, and Fewell and Gunn), then the situation is that Boaz declares that he is about to marry Ruth, not that So-and-So must do so. According to this scenario, it is this "piece of unexpected news" that caused the So-and-So "to back out of his commitment to buy the field."[104] As Nielsen explains, Boaz's announcement took everyone by surprise:

> What none of those present has so much as guessed at (nor should they have done) is Boaz's plan to marry Ruth and restore the name of Mahlon to his property. Boaz's announcement radically changes the position of the other redeemer, who had believed that he was purchasing a field from a childless widow and did not hesitate to agree to do so.[105]

This approach is rejected by the main English versions, which still strongly prefer the marginal reading, "you must buy." However, there are problems with this. Where does this obligation come from and why does So-and-So not know

---

103. This was the objection that Naboth voiced to Ahab when the king wanted to purchase his vineyard (1 Kgs 21:3).

104. Fewell and Gunn, *Compromising Redemption,* 91.

105. Nielsen, *Ruth,* 84.

about it? If we accept that Boaz announced his own intention to marry Ruth, the whole scene makes perfect sense. Boaz was warning the man that if he bought the land he should be aware that a marriage was intended. This would have implications for inheritance since if Boaz and Ruth had children that were heirs to Ruth's first husband, then the land that So-and-So was about to buy would not be inherited by his own family but by the family of Ruth and Boaz. This would have been a worrying development for So-and-So, and he decided immediately that he did not want to purchase the land if it would be inherited not by his family but by the family of Elimelech through Boaz and Ruth. Up until that stage he had only been thinking about Naomi, and it was clear that she would not have any children that could claim the land; but he had forgotten about Ruth, and this introduced a new element of risk into the deal since, if she had children, the land would ultimately belong to them. We will consider these two conflicting interpretations in more detail in the next chapter.

4:7-8 The Symbolism of a Sandal

So-and-So's refusal to redeem the land meant that the right and responsibility of redemption passed to Boaz (4:6). The transaction was confirmed by So-and-So giving his sandal to Boaz in the presence of the assembled witnesses (4:7-9). The removal of a sandal to ratify an agreement is mentioned in relation to levirate marriage in Deuteronomy, where the context is the refusal of someone to take responsibility for raising offspring for his deceased brother (Deut 25:9). However, in that context it was the widow who removed the sandal from the person who refused to marry her, and she then spat in his face. The symbolism here seems to relate to the possession of land and reflects the fact that, as Dale Manor observes, "in antiquity only the owner of a piece of property had full rights to on it."[106] There seems to have been a great deal of symbolism connected with shoes and feet, not only in Israel but also in other societies, such as Nuzi. As Hubbard explains,

> According to the Nuzi texts, for example, to validate a transfer of real estate the old owner would lift up his foot from the property and place the new owner's foot on it. In the OT, "to set foot" on the land was associated with ownership of it (Deut. 1:36; 11:24; Josh. 1:3; 14:9). Therefore, the sandal transfer in Ruth 4:7 may be a symbolic offspring of such ancient customs.[107]

106. Dale W. Manor, "Brief History of Levirate Marriage," 133.
107. Hubbard, *Ruth*, 251.

Similar symbolism is evident is Ps 60:8, where casting a sandal over a particular territory represented claiming ownership. Thus: "Moab is my washbasin; upon Edom I cast my shoe; over Philistia I shout in triumph" (ESV).

Removal of sandals was not only used in transactions, but also demanded by God or his representative on two occasions in the OT. Moses removed his sandals at the "burning bush," and Joshua carried out the same act in the presence of the commander of YHWH's army (Exod 3:4; Josh 5:15). Both Moses and Joshua were commanded to remove their sandals because they were on "holy ground." This is significant for landownership since "holy ground" is land that is set apart for the deity or, in other words, land that belongs to God. The removal of sandals by Moses and Joshua may be a humble acknowledgment that they are in the presence of deity and that they are standing on his land. In both stories landownership is a significant issue. Moses must acknowledge that Sinai is the mountain of YHWH, and he must return to that mountain with the liberated people of Israel. Joshua has crossed the Jordan and is approaching Jericho, but the city will not be inhabited by Israel — it is holy ground that belonged to the deity. Therefore, in the OT there is a close connection between ownership and sandals, and the practice explained in the book of Ruth is a further reflection of the symbolism associated with footwear.

4:9-12 The Redemption Is Confirmed and Witnessed

The transfer of the sandal signified that So-and-So had agreed to set aside his right to purchase the land from Naomi. Following this agreement, this unknown potential redeemer left the scene, and Boaz was free to act as redeemer. Apparently a crowd had gathered, and Boaz addressed the elders and "all the people" and declared that they were witnesses to his purchase of all that belonged to Elimelech and his sons, Mahlon and Kilion. He explained that he had also acquired Ruth the Moabite as his wife to perpetuate the name of her late husband, Mahlon, so that his name would not disappear from his birthplace or from his family (Ruth 4:10). Boaz was concerned that Mahlon's name be remembered. As a result of this concern, Boaz also ensured, inadvertently, that his own name would not be forgotten since he became an ancestor of King David. The second redeemer, on the other hand, acts as a foil to Boaz, because he is only remembered as So-and-So.

The witnesses were important, since apparently no written records were kept. They responded positively to Boaz and invoked a blessing that the woman entering Boaz's life would be like Rachel and Leah, the wives of Jacob who, with a little help from handmaidens, bore twelve sons and an unknown number of daughters.[108] The witnesses described Rachel and Leah as those who "together built up the house of Israel" (ESV). This description of building a house is particularly significant in relation to King David, since one of his ambitions was to build a house (temple) for YHWH. However, YHWH decreed that it would not be David but his son who would build the house. In response to David's desire to build this house, YHWH explained that he would build a house for David (a dynasty). These witnesses who referred to Rachel and Leah building the house of Israel were, of course, unaware that through the marriage that had now been agreed at the city gate, the foundations of the royal house of David were being laid.

The blessing concluded with the expression of a wish that is difficult to translate. The literal Hebrew reading is: "May you make power in Ephrathah and call a name in Bethlehem" (4:11). This idiom "make power" is translated variously: "May you act worthily" (ESV); "May you have standing" (NIV); "May you produce children" (NRSV); "Prosper" (NJPS). Hubbard suggests that in this context the idiom probably means "to acquire wealth."[109] However, it is more likely that the blessing referred to total well-being and success.

The second part of the blessing is equally ambiguous with its aspiration that Boaz will "call a name in Bethelehem." To "call a name" is an unusual phrase that probably means to be famous or influential. It recalls the promise to Abraham that God would bless him and make his name great, and, significantly, the same promise of a great name is made to David, who would come from the family line of Boaz and Ruth (Gen 12:2; 2 Sam 7:9).

The concluding invocation is that his family may be like Perez whom Tamar bore to Judah through the offspring that YHWH would give him through this young woman (Ruth 4:12). This is an acknowledgment that just as the people needed to depend on YHWH for the barley and wheat harvests, the birth of children was also a gift from him. The word used for "offspring" is עֶרַז/*zeraʿ*, literally "seed." This is an evocative description that is used frequently in Genesis. It carries the connotation that a person's life is not just an independent entity but rather it is a "seed" that has the potential to produce further seed. In Genesis God chose specific people in order that through them and through their offspring (seed) the world would be blessed. The story that began in Genesis is continued in Ruth, and the God who chose Abraham and Sarah also chose Boaz and Ruth. The reference to Judah and Tamar links Boaz and Ruth with the family that Jacob blessed when he announced, "The scepter

---

108. We are told about Dinah because of her role in the Shechem incident, but there may also have been other unmentioned daughters.

109. Hubbard, *Ruth*, 259.

shall not depart from Judah" (Gen 49:10). Perez was the son of Judah, but his mother was Tamar, a foreign woman who had been married successively to two of Judah's sons. Since both sons had died, Judah, quite illogically, blamed Tamar and refused to allow his third son to marry her. Tamar was distraught and saw that her family faced extinction. Therefore she pretended to be a prostitute and bore a son through Judah himself. Thus two foreign women, Tamar and Ruth, through their determination and commitment became important members of the family line of the tribe of Judah. That they are in the same family line as Judah is the first hint in the passage that through Boaz and Ruth the blessing promised to Judah comes one step closer to fulfillment.

4:13-17 Boaz Marries Ruth, and Obed Is Born

So at last the tension is lifted and the story reaches its denouement with the marriage of Ruth to Boaz and the birth of a son (Ruth 4:13). Just to remind the reader that this natural event was planned by God, we are told not just that Ruth conceived but also that God "gave her conception" (KJV). This may be simply a reference to the belief that children were a gift from God. However, in this context the statement is probably more significant. Ruth had been married to Mahlon for ten years without having children. Thus the reference here is to God's gracious intervention to further the special line of descendants that would lead to King David. This is a clear continuation of the theme of descendants that is so prominent in Genesis. Isaac's birth had been impossible from a human standpoint and divine intervention had been required, showing that God was indeed fulfilling his purposes through Abraham and Sarah. The divine involvement in the birth of Isaac set it aside as not only significant but also crucial to the outworking of God's plan to bless Abraham and his descendants. The reminder that God was involved throughout this story of Boaz and Ruth and that the birth of this child was enabled by him shows that the divine plan that began in Genesis is continued through this marriage of Boaz to the Moabite woman.

However, Naomi is not out of the picture. The book begins with a portrayal of her as a tragic figure who had lost everything. Who could place a value on her loss of her husband and two sons? As a result of these tragic circumstances, Naomi had described herself as "empty" and had blamed God. However, the story that introduced her as "empty" and in despair concludes on a much more positive note. The women of Bethlehem express their pleasure at what has happened to her and they bless YHWH (4:14-15). To "bless" YHWH is to praise him. The women of Bethlehem have seen a great change in Naomi since she returned from Moab in bitterness, and this gave them cause to praise God because they recognized that the changed circumstances in Naomi's life had been brought about by divine blessing. When she arrived from Moab, Naomi had blamed God for acting against her and making life unbearable. Now these women rejoiced that YHWH had not "withheld" (NJPS) a redeemer גֹּאֵל/*gō'ēl* from her (4:14). It is not clear whether the title *gō'ēl* in this passage refers to Boaz or the baby. Perhaps both are included. The verb that the NJPS translates "withheld" is from שׁבת/*šbt*, the same root as the word for "Sabbath," which means to cease from an activity. God has shown that he had not ceased from caring for Naomi and had provided a *gō'ēl* through his providential care. During the time that Naomi had been blaming God, he had not withheld his blessing from her.

The women also requested that his name be literally "called out" throughout Israel. However, there is a problem in translating this phrase because it is not clear whose name is referred to here. It could be the baby's name, as Bush suggests, and therefore a wish that he would become famous.[110] Similarly it could be a reference to Boaz. On the other hand, it could be a reference to God, such as, "May God's name be praised for all that he has done."

The women of Bethlehem highlighted the importance with which they regarded this new baby: "He shall be to you a restorer of life and a nourisher of your old age" (4:15 ESV). The phrase "restorer of life" is literally "restorer of the soul." The same vocabulary is used in the well-known terminology of Ps 23:3, where the psalmist acknowledges, "He restores my soul" (ESV). In other words, the women declared that this baby had given Naomi "a new lease on life." In her days of bitterness she had felt alone and expected to die alone and forgotten. However, now she had someone who would care for her and provide for her in old age. She would not be left alone and without support. As Bush rightly comments, the women's concern is not with the future family line of this baby, but they "are solely interested in the child because he will resolve the emptiness of Naomi's life."[111]

The women did not forget Ruth in their eulogy, and they highlighted their high regard for her and for the way that she had cared for Naomi: "for your daughter-in-law who loves you, who is more to you than seven sons" (4:15 NRSV). This was indeed a high accolade for a foreigner. Ruth's earlier title of "Ruth the Moabite" had emphasized her separate identity and her difference from Naomi and the people of Bethlehem. In this passage the women refer to her as Naomi's daughter-in-law, which highlights her acceptance not just into the family of Naomi but also into the community in Bethlehem. She was now one of them and had contributed in a special way to the happiness and

110. Bush, "Ruth," 256.
111. Ibid., 254.

fulfillment of their respected friend Naomi. This high respect and acceptance that is shown to Ruth were clearly merited. The commitment and love that she had shown to Naomi had impressed the women of Bethlehem, and they declared that Ruth was worth more than seven sons — high praise indeed in a patriarchal society. This emphasis on the value of a woman is also significant because of Naomi's earlier attitude toward life. When she was leaving Moab she made clear that she valued men above women. The only possible solution for the women was to find men and bear sons. While this was true for that society, the reference to Ruth being worth more than seven sons is a testimony against any society that values women less highly than men.

Naomi became the nurse of the baby boy (4:16). The women gave the baby the name Obed, which means "worker." Presumably this is a reference to the idea that he would be able to work on the newly redeemed land and supply the physical needs of Naomi and Ruth. Naturally, the women's focus was on the immediate practical implications and benefits of the birth of Obed, but the narrator had further information about Obed, information unknown to the characters in the story. Obed's immediate contribution to the life of Naomi and Ruth was tremendous, but his future contribution is the great highlight of the book of Ruth. Obed was the father of Jesse, who was the father of David, Israel's greatest king. The mention of David here is not just to give the account of Ruth a happy ending. The whole book is moving toward this goal. The Abraham narrative in Genesis takes us from a story of barrenness and disappointment to the birth of Isaac. His birth was nothing short of a miracle, and this highlighted that God was working out his purposes through Abraham. Naomi, like Abraham, had given up hope of having children or grandchildren. She felt abandoned and bitter and believed that her and her husband's family line was on the verge of extinction. Now, at the end of the book, the author reveals that through those dark days of desperation and despair, God was working out his plans, not just for Naomi but also for her people Israel.

Thus, in spite of its brevity and apparent insignificance, the book of Ruth presents one of the most comforting and encouraging messages of the OT. This message is one of reassurance that when we are tempted like Naomi to feel forsaken by God, to feel that he does not care, he is nevertheless still in control and will work out his purposes. The book encourages its readers not to panic during the dark times when God seems far away but to wait expectantly and to keep faith in him. This was a message that was very relevant during the exilic and early postexilic years. Many Israelites must have felt forsaken by God. Encouragement was much needed, and the book of Ruth together with passages such as Isaiah 40 and the book of Genesis would have provided a source of encouragement in those dark days.

4:18-22 Genealogical Data

The book concludes with a genealogy from Perez to David. It is introduced by the phrase, "These are the generations of," וְאֵ֣לֶּה תּוֹלְד֔וֹת/*wĕ'ēlleh tôlĕdôt*, familiar to readers of Genesis as a structuring device that divides the book into ten sections. The root of the word *tôlĕdôt* is ילד/*yld*, which means "to bear children." In Genesis the repetition of this phrase highlights the importance of the theme of offspring in that book. By contrast, the book of Ruth reaches its goal with this genealogical table. The lack of an heir has been the underlying problem for Naomi, and this short genealogy announces that Naomi's needs have been fulfilled beyond anything that she could have expected. Moreover, the genealogy reminds the reader of the activity of YHWH, who has been behind the scenes throughout the story, but as Willem Prinsloo suggests, "This genealogy, which leads up to David, is a visible proof of the abundant and continued blessing of Yahweh."[112]

The genealogy lists the names of ten men, beginning with Perez, the son of Judah, and ending with David. Comparison with the genealogy in Matthew's Gospel is interesting — Matthew includes the women Tamar, Rahab, and Ruth (1:2-6). The number ten has also appeared at the beginning of the book in the context of the ten years of tragedy and barrenness in the land of Moab (Ruth 1:4). This is balanced at the end of the book by this family tree of ten generations.

The genealogy commences with Perez, one of the twin boys born to Judah. The root of his name, פרץ/*prṣ*, occurs fairly frequently in the Hebrew Bible as a verb and as a noun. The verb refers to bursting forth, breaking through, or making a breach (Exod 19:22; 2 Sam 5:20; 1 Chr 15:13; Isa 5:5), and the noun usually implies that a breach has been made (Judg 21:15; Amos 4:3). This reflects the tradition that the midwife expected Perez's brother to be born first, but Perez at the last moment broke forth out of the womb as the firstborn. However, significantly this Hebrew root *prṣ* is also used in contexts where the focus is on blessing. For example, God's promise to Jacob at Bethel includes the assurance that his offspring will "spread abroad" (Gen 28:14), and in Exodus the reference to the exponential growth of the Israelites uses the same term (Exod 1:12). This probably explains why the genealogy begins with Perez and not Judah. This genealogy ends the book of Ruth with a family tree of those who represent the promised blessings that God made to the patriarchs. The book of Ruth begins with deprivation, death, and bitterness and ends with hope, fertility, and blessing.

112. Willem S. Prinsloo, "Theology of the Book of Ruth," 340.

Theological Horizons

Introductory Comments

Although the book of Ruth is very short and concise, it refers to many other biblical characters and alludes to theological themes that are found elsewhere. Therefore, it is important to read the book in the light of other biblical texts that have a similar theme and that mention the same characters. This includes the stories of Lot, Tamar, and Joseph. The story of David and Bathsheba and his roller-coaster relationship with Moab is also relevant. Some scholars think that the book of Ruth is intended to bring a semblance of morality into the line of David. This will be discussed below.

The value of the book of Ruth for biblical theology is far greater than we might imagine. We shall discover that not only do other texts shed light on the book of Ruth, but also Ruth makes a valuable contribution to our theological understanding of the OT.

Canonical Context

Ruth may have circulated as an individual story either in written or oral form. But now it is found as part of the canon of the OT or Hebrew Bible. By studying the book in the context of other biblical writings, we can consider how the book of Ruth fits into the bigger picture of biblical theology. Viewed in this way, the book of Ruth, far from being an independent story, is a piece in the jigsaw puzzle of the overall message of the Bible.

In the Christian canon, as in the Septuagint, the book of Ruth follows the Pentateuch, Joshua, and Judges. In the Hebrew Bible it is in the third section (the Writings) and follows the book of Proverbs. Since the book of Proverbs ends with the description of the "capable woman" (אֵשֶׁת־חַיִל/*'ēšet-ḥayil*; Prov 31:10-31) and since this same title is ascribed to Ruth (3:11), it seems appropriate that the story of Ruth should follow Proverbs.[1]

Indeed, many have accepted that the Hebrew canon reflects the original order of books and that the order in the Septuagint represents a later development. However, Tod Linafelt has challenged this view; he argues that the book of Ruth was originally written as a "connector" between Judges and 1 Samuel.[2] While we do not have enough evidence to be dogmatic about the original order of canonical books, there is merit in examining the book of Ruth in the context of the book of Judges and also in the light of the books of 1 and 2 Samuel. In this section we shall examine how Ruth relates to both Judges and Samuel and assess the extent to which the proposed relationship to these two books enhances our understanding of the short story located between them. However, we also need to take account of the many allusions in Ruth to the book of Genesis and to the implications of the laws in Deuteronomy for Ruth. So, before proceeding to the book of Judges, we shall first examine the book of Ruth in the light of Genesis and Deuteronomy.

Ruth and Genesis

The comparison between these two books yields a great deal of useful theological insight. The study of unifying themes is particularly productive. I have argued elsewhere that the theme of seed/offspring is foundational to the book of Genesis.[3] The first book of our canon may be understood as a family tree of early Israel and, in particular, of the house of David. This concept has been clearly argued and developed especially by T. D. Alexander.[4] The genealogy at the end of the book of Ruth continues the story that commenced in Genesis about the birth of Perez, the son of Judah (Gen 38:29; 46:12). In the book of Ruth the offspring of Judah are traced from Perez to David (4:18-22). Thus the genealogy of the book of Ruth may be understood as a continuation of the story about Judah's family that begins in Genesis.

There are several main themes in the book of Ruth, but the theme of offspring sets this book apart. It shows how the offspring of a Moabite became King David. Although this information is given at the end of the book,

---

1. Paul House comments that Ruth "embodies the description of the virtuous wife set forth in Proverbs 31" (*Old Testament Theology*, 455).

2. Linafelt, "Ruth," xviii.

3. James McKeown, *Genesis*, 195-218.

4. T. D. Alexander, "Seed," 769-72.

it nevertheless gives the book a sense of purpose; the book moves toward this significant declaration, and without this the book would lack not only an ending but also a theological purpose. In Genesis one can identify the theme of offspring as important because it is mentioned in every main narrative, but in the book of Ruth the significance of this theme is that it is the goal toward which the entire narrative is moving. The story of Ruth begins in the context of deprivation, misery, and death, but it ends with blessing and with a message of hope for the future.

This theme of offspring is developed in detail in Genesis, where it is clear that God singles out individuals and their families and chooses to have a close relationship with them. An intriguing feature of the Genesis narrative is that the people chosen for special blessing are usually presented in parallel with someone else who is not chosen. This allows the text to highlight the difference between the chosen character and those who have not been given this privilege. In Genesis most of the characters in the family line from Seth to Jacob are not discussed in isolation but are shadowed by another person who serves as a foil and helps to highlight the special privileges and blessing associated with being part of the special line of offspring chosen by God. By comparing the chosen person with those who are not chosen, the reader gets a clearer picture of the implications of being chosen by God. A brief survey of the development of the family tree in Genesis will show how these comparisons function to turn the spotlight on those chosen by God.

This pattern of comparisons is very clear throughout Genesis but especially in the opening chapters, where two of the characters who are compared have the same name. Thus we have two Lamechs and two Enochs. The first Lamech, Cain's descendant, boasts about murder and takes pride in his evil reputation (Gen 4:23-24). On the other hand, Lamech the descendant of Seth expresses hope for the future and longs for a reversal of the effects of the curse on the ground (4:25). Furthermore, the Cainite Lamech refers to the number seven as he boasts about revenge, but the length of his life is not given. The number seven is also significant for the Sethite Lamech, who lives for 777 years (5:31). The contrasting use of the number seven highlights the significance of revenge in the life of the faithless Lamech compared to the long life of the second Lamech, who exercised faith in naming his son Noah. The two Enochs are also contrasted in the text: the son of Cain is linked with the building of the first city (presented in Genesis as a negative and rebellious venture), while his namesake is said to "walk with God" (4:17; 5:24).

The comparisons continue in Genesis with the story of Noah. There is no personal foil for Noah, but the entire population is his foil since his faith and obedience are contrasted with the wickedness of all the other human beings around him (6:5-12). The "wickedness of the world accentuates Noah's righteousness, just as the destruction of the world highlights his survival and the significance of his close relationship with God" (6:13; 8:1).[5] In the story of the cursing of Canaan by Noah, the irreverent action of Ham provides the opportunity for the reverent act of Shem and Japheth. Canaan's curse becomes the context for the blessing of Shem and Japheth (9:22-23).

Abraham's faith, generosity, and relationship with God are accentuated by the behavior of his nephew Lot. Abraham leaves Mesopotamia as an obedient response to the call of God, but Lot simply goes with him (12:4). Abraham goes to the land that God shows him, but Lot surveys the land and chooses for himself (13:10). Lot is blessed while he remains with Abraham, but when he goes his own way, he loses everything (14:11-12). In a similar way, Genesis also contrasts Isaac with Ishmael, and Jacob with both Esau and Laban. Later, Joseph's self-control is highlighted by the actions of Reuben and Judah.[6] I develop these contrasts in more detail in my commentary on Genesis.[7]

Like the main characters in Genesis, both Boaz and Ruth have foils. Ruth's foil is Orpah. These two women are equals when they walk toward Bethlehem with Naomi. When Naomi stops and strongly advises them to go home, it is expected that both will see the wisdom of her suggestion and make the logical choice to return to Moab. This is the choice that Orpah made. It is not presented as a wrong decision, and she is not portrayed as disloyal. She makes the choice that most people would have made in her position. This natural choice made by Orpah highlights the significance and selflessness of Ruth's choice. Without any encouragement from Naomi, Ruth decided to go with her to Bethlehem even though her sister-in-law chose differently. What Ruth did was special and showed strength of character and determination. The consequence of the respective choices is that Orpah returns to Moab and forfeits the opportunity to be part of the continuing story that eventually leads to blessing, while Ruth's choice propels her into the genealogy and story line of Israel's most famous family history.

Boaz is also provided with a foil in the person known only as פְּלֹנִי אַלְמֹנִי/ *pĕlōnî 'almōnî* (So-and-So). Likewise he does nothing that is wicked or wrong in the story but simply refuses to jeopardize his family's inheritance. However, his act highlights the selflessness of Boaz, who has not given a second thought to his own inheritance and who acts for the benefit of Ruth and Naomi. This comparison between the two men ends with So-and-So leaving the scene with-

5. McKeown, *Genesis*, 207.

6. Ibid., 206-9.

7. Ibid., passim.

out even his name being remembered, while Boaz enters the family tree of King David.

Naomi's foil is herself. We have a comparison between Naomi in her bitterness and Naomi when her faith is restored. In bitterness she had only complaints and lacked initiative, but when she realized that God has not forgotten about her, in her restored faith she took the initiative and acted very differently. The contrast between these two portrayals of Naomi testifies to the importance of faith and to the difference that it can make in a person's life.

It is also possible that the characters in Ruth are consciously being compared with other well-known characters. Ruth's selfless decision to leave her home and her relatives is presented in a way that invites a comparison with Abraham. Thus Boaz reminds her: "You left your father and mother and your homeland and came to live with a people you did not know before" (Ruth 2:11 NIV). This reflects the similar language in the call of Abraham: "Leave your country, your people, and your father's household and go to the land I will show you" (Gen 12:1 NIV). Like the patriarch, Ruth left her homeland and family; but whereas the patriarch was encouraged and motivated by divine promises, Ruth was apparently motivated mainly by love and concern for her mother-in-law. Thus by comparing Ruth and Abraham, the author accentuates the enormity of the choice that she made. Furthermore, the separation between Abraham and Lot (the father of the Moabites) provides an interesting context in which to understand the commitment of Ruth to Naomi. Lot was willing to separate from his uncle Abraham; but unlike Lot, Ruth refused to be separated from the one she loved (see the commentary on Ruth 1:14-18).

Yitzhak Berger also compares the journey to Bethlehem during which the two women walk together (Ruth 1:19) with the story of Abraham and Isaac in Gen 22:6, 8, where Abraham and Isaac "walk together" toward the place where Abraham has been told to sacrifice his son. Isaac walked with Abraham, just as Ruth walked with Naomi, both of them walking toward an unknown future. Berger argues that "Ruth's personal sacrifice might be seen to rival that of Isaac and provide an early signal of her emergence as a mother in Israel equivalent to the nation's ancestral founders."[8]

Further light is shed on the characters in Ruth when we study them within the interpretive framework established in the book of Genesis. In Genesis there is continual repetition of the motif that the person chosen by God is often *not* the most likely choice from a human standpoint — not the firstborn and not without flaws. God chooses Abel, not Cain, even though Cain was the firstborn. This theme continues with the choice of Abraham, not Nahor; Isaac, not Ish-

---

8. Yitzhak Berger, "Ruth and Inner-Biblical Allusion," 255-56.

mael; Jacob, not Esau; Joseph, not Reuben. It is also worth mentioning in this context that God appeared to Hagar but not to Sarah. Ultimately God chose unlikely people throughout the book of Genesis.

This choice of unlikely people is obviously an important theme in the book of Ruth. The main characters in the story, Ruth and Boaz, are both unlikely choices as the ancestors of King David: Boaz was not the closest relative to Elimelech and Ruth was a foreigner from Moab. In the light of the stormy relationship between Moab and Israel, Ruth the Moabite must rank as one of the most unlikely people to become the ancestress of King David. However, even David himself was not an obvious choice. When Samuel tells Jesse that one of his sons will be king, he does not even invite David to meet Samuel. He was not even on Jesse's short list as a possible king of Israel (1 Sam 16:5-13). The theological message from all this is a warning not to despise people who do not fit our stereotypes. God's system of values is not influenced by racial prejudice or the order in which people are born.

Thus the theme of offspring in the book of Ruth provides the book with its main story line, and it also shows affinity with the same theme in the book of Genesis. This is particularly evident in the way that both books reach the same denouement. Genesis points forward to the prominence of the tribe of Judah as the royal tribe, and the book of Ruth traces the genealogy of the tribe's most famous king to a woman from the land of Moab.

It is not only the theme of seed/offspring that relates Ruth to Genesis but also the themes of land and blessing. The book of Ruth reflects the fulfillment of the promises to Abraham of blessing in the land that God provided. It also highlights the same tension as Genesis in that the land flowing with milk and honey was prone to severe famines.

Berger has drawn attention to many further allusions in the book of Ruth to Genesis. For example, Ruth 2:20 and Gen 24:27 are both passages that relate to the providence of God. In the Genesis story, the servant of Abraham acknowledges God's guidance and help in his search for a bride for Isaac. In the book of Ruth, Naomi acknowledges that in spite of her earlier bitterness, God was indeed working on their behalf. Significantly, the same words of praise are found in both passages but nowhere else in the Bible: both the servant and Naomi acknowledged the help of God, אֲשֶׁר לֹא־עָזַב חַסְדּוֹ/*'ăšer lō'-'āzab ḥasdô,* "who had not stopped showing his steadfast love" (Gen 24:27; Ruth 2:20; my trans.).[9]

Berger draws attention not just to similarities but also to contrasts between Ruth and Genesis. For example, in Genesis Abraham goes to Egypt be-

9. Ibid., 256.

cause there is a famine in the land and he returns to Canaan with great riches. However, although Naomi also leaves the land for the same reason as Abraham, she returns home empty-handed![10]

Thus the connection between Ruth and Genesis fulfills multiple purposes. However, as Tamara Eskenazi points out, the book of Ruth also functions to "right wrongs — redeeming, as it were, things gone awry in Genesis."[11] Harold Fisch also mentions this idea of the book of Ruth "redeeming" the earlier episodes such as the Lot and Abraham stories. Referring back to the Genesis stories, he comments,

> The Ruth-Boaz story is the means of "redeeming" the entire corpus and of asserting it into the pattern of *Heilsgeschichte*. Ruth establishes a new kind of language for understanding what has gone before, so that a full exegesis of the stories of Lot and Judah requires reference to the story of Ruth and, conversely, the story of Ruth looks back to these earlier paradigms and forward to what is to be disclosed in the story of the house of David.[12]

Thus the story of Ruth is enriched when we see it in its wider context as part of the story that spans from Genesis through Kings.

Further possible points of contact between Ruth and Genesis will be dealt with in the following sections relating to biblical themes, especially "Providence and Guidance" and "Land."

Ruth and Deuteronomy

Deuteronomy has two main implications for the book of Ruth — one positive and one negative. The positive implication comes from the encouragement to love the foreigner.

> For the LORD your God is God of gods and Lord of lords, the great God, mighty and awesome, who shows no partiality and accepts no bribes.
>
> He defends the cause of the fatherless and the widow, and loves the foreigner residing among you, giving them food and clothing. And you are to love those who are foreigners, for you yourselves were foreigners in Egypt (Deut 10:17-19 NIV).

10. Ibid.
11. Eskenazi and Frymer-Kensky, *Ruth,* xxi.
12. Harold Fisch, "Ruth," 436.

The story of Ruth provides a good illustration of the practice of this Deutero-nomic call to love the foreigner. Ruth was shown respect, given food, protected, and eventually accepted into the Israelite community through marriage.

However, Deuteronomy has also a negative implication for the book of Ruth and raises questions about the acceptance of a Moabite by Israelites.

> No Ammonite or Moabite may enter the assembly of the Lord. Even to the tenth generation, none of them may enter the assembly of the Lord forever, because they did not meet you with bread and with water on the way, when you came out of Egypt, and because they hired against you Balaam the son of Beor from Pethor of Mesopotamia, to curse you. But the Lord your God would not listen to Balaam; instead the Lord your God turned the curse into a blessing for you, because the Lord your God loved you. You shall not seek their peace or their prosperity all your days forever. (Deut 23:3-6 ESV)

This passage is difficult to reconcile with the story of Ruth. The Targum rec-ognizes the problem and addresses it in the first conversation between Ruth and Boaz:

> And she [Ruth] prostrated herself with her face to the ground. And she said to him, "Why have I found favor in your eyes, to acknowledge me, when I am of a foreign people, from the daughters of Moab, who are not permitted to enter into the congregation of the Lord?" Boaz said in reply, "I have been surely told about the edict of the sages: that when the Lord commanded concerning you, he commanded only in reference to the males." (2:11)[13]

This tension between Deuteronomy 23 and the book of Ruth may even be reflected in the text itself. Eskenazi and Frymer-Kenski comment, "This tension helps explain the kinds of maneuvering that first Naomi and then Boaz engage in before Boaz announces his intention to marry Ruth: the obstacle blocking their union is Ruth's Moabite status, the proverbial elephant in the room."[14] Thus the tension between Deuteronomy and Ruth may be a deliberate motif in the text showing how the love for the foreigner, stipulated by Deuteronomy, took precedence over the exclusion clause found in the same book.

---

13. Levine, *Aramaic Version of Ruth*, 26, 72-76.
14. Eskenazi and Frymer-Kensky, *Ruth*, xxiii.

Ruth and Judges

As mentioned above, in the Hebrew canon the book of Ruth is found in the third section known as the "Writings," but most English translations follow the Septuagint and place the book of Ruth after the book of Judges. A close relationship between the books of Judges and Ruth is indicated by the first verse of Ruth, which locates the story of the book in the period of the judges. To grasp fully the theological message of the book of Ruth, it is helpful to familiarize ourselves with the content and main theological themes of Judges.

Part of Israel's problem was the lack of leadership, and during the judges period "everyone did what was right in his own eyes" (Judg 21:25). The book of Judges looks forward to a time when a king would lead the nation, and in particular it anticipates the future reign of King David. Although Israel's first kings, Saul and David, are not mentioned in the book of Judges, the book highlights the importance of the tribe of Judah and details the disastrous history of the tribe of Benjamin, which is an indication that future hope lay with the king from the tribe of Judah rather than with the Benjaminite who preceded him. Evidence for David and not Saul as the ideal that the book of Judges looked forward to is found in the different portrayals of the tribes of Judah and Benjamin. The tribe of Judah was the first to claim its territory with divine approval (Judg 1:2). On the other hand, the reports about the tribe of Benjamin describe idolatry, violence, and desperation. This is exemplified in the story of the Levite who received good hospitality at Bethlehem, where David was born, but his concubine was murdered at Gibeah, where Saul was born (Judg 19:1-30). Eugene Merrill highlights the emphasis on Bethlehem in both Judges and Ruth and refers to the "so-called Bethlehem trilogy," made up of the stories in Judges 17–18, 19–21, and the book of Ruth.[15] Merrill observes that these three stories hold in common the motif of a man leaving Bethlehem; but whereas in the book of Judges the "two men sullied the reputation of the town by their subsequent behavior, Elimelech and his family enhanced it."[16] Merrill concludes that "Saul's ancestors had humiliated and disgraced a Bethlehemite, much to their chagrin to be sure, but Bethlehem not only survived this but went on to produce Saul's successor, the man after God's own heart."[17] In its anticipation of the reign of David, the book of Judges leads smoothly and seamlessly to the book of Ruth. Like the book of Judges, the genealogy at the end of Ruth points to David, the future king of Israel.

---

15. Eugene H. Merrill, "Book of Ruth," 131. This approach is followed by Reg Grant, "Literary Structure in Ruth," 426.

16. Merrill, "Book of Ruth," 132.

17. Ibid., 133.

There are also contrasts between the book of Ruth and the book of Judges in relation to how the books portray the treatment of women. An apt title for the book of Judges would be, "Men Behaving Badly." John Goldingay published a book with this title, but he found enough men behaving badly in Samuel–Kings and did not include the book of Judges! Relationships between men and women are frequently highlighted in the book of Judges. Many women are mentioned, but most of them are treated merely as someone else's property and only a few are named. Caleb offered his daughter Achsah in marriage to any man who could capture Kiriath-sepher (Judg 1:12). The town was captured by Caleb's younger brother Othniel. Achsah asked her husband to persuade her father to give her a field. She then approached her father directly for springs of water, and he gave her "the upper and lower springs." Achsah is mentioned three times in the Bible, presumably because she showed determination and courage to provide for the future in difficult circumstances (Josh 15:16-19 par. Judg 1:12-15; 1 Chr 2:49). Her husband became the first judge of Israel, but Achsah is also portrayed as resourceful and successful in spite of the disadvantage of living in a society dominated by men. Ruth, in many ways, showed similar strength of character and resolve as Achsah, and both women are celebrated in the books of Judges and Ruth for their resilience and resourcefulness. It is noteworthy that whereas Achsah had no choice about whom she should marry, Ruth was free to choose. Moreover, the second mention of women in the book of Judges is a record of women being given and taken as wives (Judg 3:6). The story of Ruth is about a woman who would reverse this trend and propose marriage at the threshing floor, rather than wait to be "taken."

Israel had only one female judge — Deborah. She fulfilled that role in a different way than the men in that she acted as a counselor and prophetess. She did not lead the Israelites into battle herself but commissioned Barak to fulfill this role. He stipulated that she must go with him, and this leads to her riposte that Sisera will be killed by a woman (Judg 4). In the same story and in fulfillment of Deborah's prediction, Jael the Kenite killed Sisera by deceiving him and giving him a false sense of security in her tent. Her violent act delivered Israel from its enemies (4:21). Both Deborah and Jael are recognized as resourceful and determined. We should also note that Jael, like Ruth, is not an Israelite, although her tribe was related to Israel through Moses' marriage to the daughter of Jethro (1:16). The story of the defeat of the Canaanites ends with the ironic insight into the expectations of the mother of Sisera and her wisest princesses (5:28-30 NIV):

> Through the window peered Sisera's mother;
>   behind the lattice she cried out,

"Why is his chariot so long in coming?
Why is the clatter of his chariots delayed?"
The wisest of her ladies answer her;
indeed, she keeps saying to herself.
"Are they not finding and dividing the spoils:
a woman or two for each man?"

The words of these "wise" princesses highlight the brutal treatment of women in the aftermath of war; unlike Deborah, their predictions were just wishful thinking and their hopes were dashed.

No women are mentioned by name in the story of Gideon, but we are told that he had many wives who bore seventy sons for him (8:30). Presumably he had many daughters, but they are not mentioned. As well as his wives, he had an unnamed concubine who bore a son called Abimelech (8:31). The only reference to a woman in Abimelech's career, apart from his mother, relates to the woman who killed him. However, his attitude is clearly revealed in his request that it should not be said that a woman killed him (9:53-54). The woman is called "a certain woman" (ESV). His attitude to women is clearly very different from the attitude of Boaz in the book of Ruth.

Jephthah was the son of a prostitute. His brothers called him the "son of another woman" (11:2 ESV) and drove him out. Jephthah's vow and his relationship to his daughter are strange and disturbing (11:29-40). However, Jephthah's daughter's dignified response is in sharp contrast to her father's rashness and folly.

The angel of YHWH appeared to Manoah's wife (13:3-5). Manoah prayed that the angel would return and instruct them how to raise this special child. One more time the angel appeared to the woman and she ran and told her husband. In the context of the book of Judges with its continual mistreatment of women, it is very significant that the angel of YHWH appeared twice to a woman but not to her husband.

Samson's exploits are well known, particularly those with women. He justifies his decision to marry a Philistine because "she is right (יָשְׁרָה/*yāšrâ*) in my eyes" (14:3 ESV). This is a clear reflection of the repeated refrain at the end of the book of Judges that "everyone did what was right (הַיָּשָׁר/*hayyāšār*) in his own eyes" (17:6; 21:25). At the same time the providence of God is also given as a reason for Samson's behavior since God was seeking an opportunity to harm the Philistines, who ruled Israel at that time (14:4).

Samson's behavior at his wedding party placed an unbearable strain on his relationship with his Philistine wife and with his companions at the wedding feast. His behavior led to his wife marrying his best man and to many Philistines being slaughtered by an angry, vindictive Samson. The Philistines, who matched Samson in their ruthlessness, burned his wife and her family, inviting further retaliation from Samson (Judg 14–15). Later, an encounter with a prostitute in Gaza led Samson into a trap from which he easily escaped, but his encounter with the treacherous Delilah proved to be his downfall. Following his death, we are told that he judged Israel for twenty years (Judg 16:31).

Samson is the last judge mentioned in the book, but the treatment of women remains an important issue in the remaining chapters. The crime against the concubine in chapter 19 and the way in which she was murdered by the Benjaminites is a particularly harrowing account that led to civil war among the tribes. The final chapter relates to finding wives for the men of Benjamin.

Thus men are in charge in the judges period, but some of the wisest decisions and the bravest acts are carried out by women. However, the book of Judges also bears witness to a time when women were taken for granted and much abusive treatment is recorded. As Adrien Bledstein points out, the use or abuse of women is "a motif underlying nearly every episode in the book of Judges."[18]

When we understand the book of Ruth against the background of the book of Judges, its message becomes even more meaningful and rich. While there were women around like Delilah, scheming and dangerous, the book of Ruth provides a much more attractive picture of ordinary women caught up in a crisis. Their skill at survival and their humble dependence on others are all the more poignant in the light of the generally low moral tone that prevails in the book of Judges.

A further link between the two books is made by the different roles played by the land of Moab. One of the judges (Ehud) led Israel against the Moabites (3:15-30). Eglon the king of Moab is an object of derision because he was so obese that the sword that Ehud used to kill him disappeared into his abdomen (3:29). The story goes on to describe how the Israelites killed ten thousand men of Moab. Following this catalogue of bloodshed, the book of Ruth reassures the reader that these stories of aggression and war were not the full story. An entirely different interaction between Moab and Israel is portrayed in the account of people from Bethlehem finding sustenance in Moab and a Moabite widow finding refuge, friendship, and marriage in Israel.

Moreover, there is an interesting variation in the way that the Hebrew word חַיִל/*ḥayil* ("valor") is used in the book of Ruth compared to Judges. This term is applied to warriors in Judges, not only to Israelites but also to the fighting men of Moab, and each one is described as אִישׁ חַיִל/*'îš ḥayil* — "man of

18. Adrien J. Bledstein, "Female Companionships," 117.

valor, able-bodied man" (Judg 3:29; 20:44, 46; cf. 18:2). Gideon and Jephthah are referred to as חַיִל גִּבּוֹר/*gibbôr ḥayil,* which is stronger than *'îš ḥayil* and is usually translated "mighty man of valor" (Judg 6:12 ESV). Thus although the term *ḥayil* is used to describe trained soldiers, the term *gibbôr ḥayil* is used to describe the two heroes Gideon and Jephthah. Indeed, this same title is used as a description of Boaz and may refer to his success and wealth rather than to any military prowess (Ruth 2:1).[19] Although *ḥayil* is almost exclusively regarded as a male trait, it is also used of Ruth, who is described as חַיִל אֵשֶׁת/*'ēšet ḥayil* by Boaz (3:11). The term probably refers to her ability to succeed even in the most difficult circumstances, and it is translated as "worthy woman" (NRSV, ESV), "virtuous woman" (KJV, NLT), "woman of noble character" (NIV). The other occasion when this term refers to a woman is in the book of Proverbs, where it occurs twice in relation to the wife of noble character (Prov 12:4; 31:10). Thus the term that is used in the book of Judges to describe brave fighting men is used in Ruth as a description of both Boaz and Ruth because of their commitment and love rather than because of their skill on the battlefield.

In conclusion, it is clear that the book of Ruth takes on an added dimension when we consider it in the light of the book of Judges. Alicia Ostriker provides the following helpful summary of the contrasting content of these two books:

> Judges is a book of relentless violence, slaughter and war, external and internal. It also contains the horrific stories of Jephthah's daughter and the Levite's concubine, and is a perfect illustration of the idea that a militarized society is a bad thing for women. If the text of Judges is warfare, its subtext is gender war. Ruth, in sharp contrast, is a pastoral. It occurs in peacetime, its plot does not turn on conflict, its values have nothing to do with conquest and killing but with personal and family relationships, fertility and ongoing life.[20]

The military and nationalistic focus of the book of Judges is appropriately balanced and nuanced by the family focus of the book of Ruth. Ruth's story of loyalty and love provide the reader with a refreshing literary oasis that is very welcome after the shocking content of the book of Judges. As Block states, "after the Book of Judges the Book of Ruth offers the reader welcome relief."[21]

19. This term חַיִל גִּבּוֹר/*gibbôr ḥayil* is also used in relation to Kish the father of Saul (1 Sam 9:1). Since he is not described as a soldier, the term may refer to his wealth and standing in the community.

20. Alicia Ostriker, "Book of Ruth," 346.

21. Block, "Ruth," 588.

Ruth and the Books of Samuel

As we have seen, the book of Ruth clearly alludes to the books of Genesis and Judges. However, the book also looks forward to the reign of King David (Ruth 4:18-22). The book of Ruth ends in the Hebrew Bible and also in most English translations with the name "David." Linafelt observes that all the other genealogies in the Bible introduce a story rather than conclude it; and, he comments,

> Unless one takes Ruth as the only exception to this otherwise quite consistent feature of genealogies, one must assume that the ending of Ruth actually functions to open out to another story. And the most natural story to follow a genealogical list that leads to the name of David would be the story of David's succession to the throne of Israel, told in the books of Samuel.[22]

Thus by ending with this genealogy the book of Ruth is not a completed story but points forward to the life of David as described in 1 and 2 Samuel.

Berger has observed further connections between Ruth and Samuel. He draws attention to possible allusions in the book of Ruth to the story of Abigail and David in 1 Samuel 25. Nabal, Abigail's husband, is introduced in a similar way to Elimelech, and then his death is also recorded, as is that of Elimelech in the book of Ruth. Berger traces several verbal parallels between the two stories. For example, Ruth lies at Boaz's feet and Abigail falls at David's feet, and "Boaz and David each marry the widow who prompted him to do the right thing."[23] This comparison between the story of Ruth and the story of Abigail is interesting because the story line is similar. Ruth and David both required food: Ruth for herself and Naomi, David for himself and his men, who were fleeing from Saul. The similarities in the story line enable us to compare and contrast the attitude and motivation of the characters. On the one hand, Ruth humbly requested permission to glean in the field, which was her right as a poor person. When she received more than she asked for from Boaz, she responded with humility and gratitude. On the other hand, David asked for food from Nabal, but when it was refused he responded with threats of violence and fully intended to take revenge. These contrasts show Ruth in a much more favorable light than her great-grandson, King David. There are also comparisons between the roles of Abigail and Ruth. Both women took drastic initiatives in order to influence powerful men, and both succeeded admirably. However, it is interesting that Berger views Abigail in a negative light, describing her as "David's scheming

22. Linafelt, "Ruth," xx.
23. Berger, "Ruth and Inner-Biblical Allusion," 259.

accomplice." He contrasts the character of Ruth with that of Abigail and concludes that the "moral integrity of a young woman from Moab" is highlighted by "the shady machinations of the wife of Nabal."

> David's marriage to Abigail enables him to usurp power, even murderously, while she — to one extent or another — acts as a scheming accomplice. In sharp contrast, the restraint and integrity displayed by Ruth when seeking Boaz's hand in marriage set a moral standard for kings of Israel, who now inevitably rise from the Moabite convert's own progeny.[24]

This characterization of Abigail as David's scheming accomplice is open to question. She was reacting to a very challenging situation. She and Ruth were responding to different circumstances, and perhaps they have more in common than Berger suggests. Both showed practical wisdom enabling them to survive in difficult circumstances.

However, the relationship between Boaz and Ruth is certainly a commentary on how David's relationship with the opposite sex was open to criticism. The respect and dignity that Boaz showed toward Ruth is in sharp contrast with the way that David treated women. In our comparison between Genesis and Ruth, we saw how the book of Ruth provided a corrective to the wrongs committed in Genesis. In much the same way, Ruth provides a commentary on the behavior of King David. David's behavior in relation to Bathsheba shows Israel's greatest king as a very poor role model, whereas Boaz's behavior was exemplary (2 Sam 11:1-27).[25]

The book of Ruth also draws attention to David's relationship with Moab (see the section "The Land of Moab" in the next chapter). At first his relationship was good, and the Moabites had provided refuge for David's parents when they were in danger (1 Sam 22:3-4). But unexpectedly David treated Moabite prisoners with extreme brutality: "And he defeated Moab and he measured them with a line, making them lie down on the ground. Two lines he measured to be put to death, and one full line to be spared. And the Moabites became servants to David and brought tribute" (2 Sam 8:2 ESV). No reason is given in the text for this behavior, and the narrator does not excuse it. David repaid the Moabites' kindness to his parents with bloodshed. The book of Ruth highlights the seriousness of David's war crimes in much the same way as Nathan's parable rebukes him for his affair with Bathsheba.

---

24. Ibid., 267-69.
25. See Fisch, "Ruth," 436.

The Marriage of Ruth

Many assume that the ancient custom known as *levirate marriage* provides the context and helps to explain the circumstances behind the marriage of Ruth to Boaz. In this section we shall examine this custom and look at the main arguments for and against the theory that the marriage in the book of Ruth belongs to this category.[26]

Levirate marriage was a convention whereby the brother of a dead man was obliged to marry his widow. Furthermore, the widow herself was legally required to marry her husband's brother and she was forbidden to marry someone outside her husband's family. The term *levirate* is from Latin, and the related noun *levir* means "brother-in-law." This is a translation of Hebrew יָבָם/ *yābām,* which also refers to a husband's brother. The corresponding Hebrew verb means to fulfill the duty of a brother-in-law. References to this custom are found in Gen 38:8 and Deut 25:5-10. It was also an issue at the time of Jesus (Matt 22:23-28).

The text of Deut 25:5-10 (ESV) is as follows:

> If brothers dwell together, and one of them dies and has no son, the wife of the dead man shall not be married outside the family to a stranger. Her husband's brother shall go in to her and take her as his wife and perform the duty of a husband's brother to her. And the first son whom she bears shall succeed to the name of his dead brother, that his name may not be blotted out of Israel. And if the man does not wish to take his brother's wife, then his brother's wife shall go up to the gate to the elders and say, "My husband's brother refuses to perpetuate his brother's name in Israel; he will not perform the duty of a husband's brother to me." Then the elders of his city shall call him and speak to him, and if he persists, saying, "I do not wish to take her," then his brother's wife shall go up to him in the presence of the elders and pull his sandal off his foot and spit in his face. And she shall answer and say, "So shall it be done to the man who does not build up his brother's house." And the name of his house shall be called in Israel, "The house of him who had his sandal pulled off."

This passage applies specifically to a situation where two or more brothers "dwell together." If one of the brothers dies, his widow would now be vulnerable and would need support. Significantly, however, the customs were not only for the widow's benefit but also to perpetuate the name and heritage of her

---

26. There is an excellent discussion of levirate marriage by Bush, "Ruth," 221-25.

dead husband so that the name of the deceased "may not be blotted out from Israel" (25:6). However, if the man refused to marry his brother's widow, then a ceremony was held during which the brother was required to announce his refusal in public before the elders at the city gate (25:8). The widow would then walk up to him, pull off one of his sandals, and spit in his face.

The other passage in the OT that mentions levirate marriage is Genesis 38. This is the account of the marriage of Jacob's son Judah to a Canaanite wife, Shua, who bore three children — Er, Onan, and Shelah. Judah selected a wife for Er about whom we are told nothing except her name — Tamar. Tamar, like her mother-in-law, was probably a Canaanite, but her nationality is not an issue in the story. Er died before any children were born, and his death is recorded as divine judgment in response to his wickedness (38:6-7). Then, in accordance with the levirate custom, the widow of the deceased became the wife of his brother Onan. The objective of this union was to "raise up offspring for your brother" (38:8). Onan, however, rebelled against his duty and refused to have offspring that would not be his own. This neglect of duty resulted in divine retribution and death (38:10). Now, according to the levirate custom, the third son, Shelah, should have married Tamar. However, since marriage to Tamar apparently had fatal consequences for two of his sons, Judah was not willing to allow his third son to take this risk. Therefore, using the pretext that Shelah was too young to marry, Judah deceptively told Tamar to go back to her "father's house" and wait until Shelah was old enough for marriage (38:11). Eventually, it became obvious to Tamar that Judah had no intention of fulfilling his promise, and she devised her own devious method to have children. Pretending to be a prostitute, she bore twins to her father-in-law Judah — Perez and Zerah.

Perhaps the stipulations in Deuteronomy were designed to protect widows like Tamar. According to Deuteronomy, if a brother refused to fulfill his obligation, his brother's widow had the opportunity to take legal action and to declare in a public ceremony that he had not fulfilled his duty. Presumably this ceremony gave the widow the right to marry outside the family that had now rejected her and thus avoid the waiting and uncertainty that Judah had imposed on Tamar. So in both Deuteronomy 25 and Genesis 38, the underlying supposition is that the widow is expected to marry the next eligible brother, and only if he refuses can she marry someone else.

The question that scholars have discussed at length is whether the story of Ruth's marriage is an example of the kind of levirate marriage that is enacted in Genesis and described in Deuteronomy. There are similarities since her husband had died and the new marriage was to a near kinsman. Together they raised a child in the name of the person who died. This was indeed the purpose of the levirate custom. The problem as stated by A. A. Anderson is that "some points of our evidence seem to require a levirate interpretation, e.g. Ruth iv. 5, 10, while other data militate against such an interpretation."[27]

What, then, are difficulties with the levirate interpretation? In particular, the levirate custom as described in Deuteronomy is specifically related to "brothers who dwell together." In Deuteronomy the *levir* must be not just a kinsman but a blood brother. However, one suggestion is that the book of Ruth shows that the levirate custom was widened to include not just immediate brothers but also other kinsmen. Thus Donald Leggett comments, "The Book of Ruth, then, shows that the levirate law of Deuteronomy has been extended in both its subjects and objects. The obligation of marrying a childless widow concerned all relatives and operated in order of their degree of relationship."[28]

While this approach is interesting and resolves some of the problems, I do not find it convincing since it rests on the presupposition that the marriage was levirate and then seeks to explain why it does not have the appearance of a levirate marriage by postulating that the regulations must have changed. Thus this argument seems circular and does not provide any evidence that the marriage was levirate but simply assumes so. Thomas and Dorothy Thompson recognized this problem but nevertheless accepted that Boaz's marriage to Ruth was a levirate marriage. They maintained that the differences between the account in Ruth and the laws in Deuteronomy are not a serious problem since both passages uphold the same Israelite values. They argued that the laws in Deuteronomy should not be interpreted in a legalistic manner but should be understood as a "statement of general principles and traditions according to which the elders would make any necessary judgments."[29] However, this seems to miss the point that the stipulation that these regulations apply to "brothers living together" does not appear as an incidental detail but as the essential circumstance that gives rise to the regulations.

Understanding Ruth's marriage in the light of levirate custom is therefore very problematic since this institution was specifically related to a family situation where brothers were living together. The institution was designed primarily to protect the land of the deceased and to make provision for the widow following her husband's death. Levirate custom operated by imposing an obligation on the next eligible brother to marry the widow, and there was a similar obligation imposed on the widow herself to marry within the family. In Ruth's marriage there is no outright obligation, and Boaz is not the brother of Mahlon. Furthermore, according to the levirate customs, not only was the

---

27. A. A. Anderson, "Marriage of Ruth," 173.

28. Leggett, *Levirate and Goel Institutions,* 245.

29. Thomas and Dorothy Thompson, "Some Legal Problems," 89.

eligible brother under obligation to marry the widow, but also the widow herself seems to have had no choice in the matter. However, it is clear that the limitations to marry within the family do not apply to Ruth since she is free to marry without any reference to her dead husband. This is what would have happened if she had stayed in Moab, and this is also the clear implication of Boaz's gratitude to her that she had not gone after younger men.

There are obvious links between the story of the levirate marriage in Genesis 38 and the marriage of Ruth: the people involved in the story in Genesis are mentioned by name in the book of Ruth — Judah, Tamar, and Perez (Ruth 4:12). However, the connection should be seen more as a contrast than as a comparison. The characters in Genesis failed to keep their obligation to Tamar, and she was treated deplorably and had to feign prostitution in order to produce offspring. Furthermore, she apparently had no other option open to her, since just as Judah was under obligation to give his son to her in marriage, she was under obligation to wait for him. Judah was not able to provide an alternative for Tamar, and yet he did not give her the liberty to marry an outsider. Instead, he cruelly kept her waiting for the son whom he had no intention of giving to her. By waiting in this way she fulfilled her obligation and only acted surreptitiously when Judah failed to keep his promise. Neither Ruth nor Boaz had any obligation to one another. Indeed, he praised her for not marrying someone else, and he is portrayed as a man of valor because of the role he played. They acted without obligation to fulfill the same objectives that levirate law fulfilled. However, their lack of obligation removes their marriage from this category.

In Genesis Tamar has a child by her father-in-law because she was not permitted to marry her late husband's brother. Dale Manor discusses the possibility that the "Genesis record could be reflecting the custom from an age when the father-in-law was a legitimate 'levirate' if he had no further sons."[30] While this is possible, it is unlikely, since as Manor points out, "Judah still had a son, Shelah, whom he could have given to Tamar for the levirate relation (Gen. 38:11, 14, 26)."[31] Furthermore, Tamar's relationship with her father-in-law Judah was out of desperation on her part, and it was done in ignorance on his part. Moreover, they did not get married, and the sons who were born from this union were described as Judah's sons (46:12); but if they had been considered as levirate offspring, they would have been acknowledged as the sons of Tamar's first husband. This account in the book of Genesis shows a breakdown in the levirate custom, and the desperate attempt of Tamar to have children, even through her father-in-law, did not conform to the legal provisions of levirate

---

30. Dale W. Manor, "Brief History of Levirate Marriage," 135.
31. Ibid.

law. Thus the Tamar/Judah story cannot be used to show that someone other than a brother could fulfill the levirate duties.

The levirate law was also known in NT times. An incident is recorded in Matt 22:23-28 in which the Sadducees challenged Jesus with the following conundrum:

> The same day Sadducees came to him, who say that there is no resurrection, and they asked him a question, saying, "Teacher, Moses said, 'If a man dies having no children, his brother must marry the widow and raise up children for his brother.' Now there were seven brothers among us. The first married and died, and having no children left his wife to his brother. So too the second and third, down to the seventh. After them all, the woman died. In the resurrection, therefore, of the seven, whose wife will she be? For they all had her." (ESV)

Thus in this NT passage, as in all references to levirate customs in the OT, only brothers are involved. Why then do scholars so readily assume that the levirate laws have anything to do with the marriage of Ruth? A very tenuous assumption seems to be made that somehow the levirate laws changed to include relatives as well as brothers. There is no evidence for this assumption. Furthermore, the levirate system involved an obligation, and if a brother did not accept that obligation he was to be publicly shamed. Without doubt, the two key elements in the levirate custom were that those involved were brothers and that a serious and binding obligation was placed upon them. Levirate marriage was first and foremost an obligation that could not be lightly ignored. The implication of this is that we should understand Ruth in terms of redemption, not levirate marriage.

However, the interesting incident of the transfer of a sandal between So-and-So and Boaz seems at first to link the incident to levirate custom. In Deut 25:9 the woman who had been rejected by her brother-in-law could "pull his sandal off his foot and spit in his face." In Ruth a sandal is also involved (Ruth 4:8). However, the customs are clearly very different. No one spits in So-and-So's face, and the removal of the sandal is not performed by the widow concerned. Josephus, however, who believed that this was a levirate marriage, added details to the story of Ruth to make it conform to the pattern in Deuteronomy. According to Josephus, Ruth was present at the gate, and when So-and-So refused to marry her, she "loosened the man's shoe and spit in his face, as the law required."[32] However, in the biblical text of Ruth, the other redeemer is not

---

32. Josephus, *Antiquities* 5.335. Translation of Paul L. Maier, *Josephus*, 98.

condemned for his actions and the transfer of the sandal seems to relate to the deal concerning the land, not to the marriage of Ruth. As Manor observes, the "sandal ceremony serves as further indication that this is not simply a levirate concern."[33] The practice of the sandal transfer probably related only to the transfer of ownership of the land, and reflects the fact that, as Manor observes, "in antiquity only the owner of a piece of property had full rights to walk on it."[34]

In the light of this connection between footwear and ownership of property, it is probable that the transfer of the sandal signified that So-and-So had agreed to set aside his right to purchase the land from Naomi. Following this agreement, this unknown potential redeemer leaves the scene and Boaz is free to act as redeemer by purchasing the land.

Thus Manor is correct that "the Ruth narrative does not seem to be a case of strict levirate marriage."[35] Hubbard reaches a stronger conclusion: "a true levirate marriage is impossible."[36] Anderson also argues convincingly that the marriage of Ruth was not a levirate marriage,[37] for Naomi was unaware of such a possibility. She thought there was no hope of Ruth and Orpah getting husbands in Bethlehem, and she urged them to return to their homes and marry Moabite men.[38] If Naomi had known that the close relatives in Bethlehem would be obliged to marry Ruth, she certainly did not divulge this; indeed, the story of Ruth derives its tension from the underlying assumption that if God had not been controlling events, Ruth would not have married Boaz. Although many have read the levirate customs into the book of Ruth, it is most unlikely that this custom is in any way related to the story. The strength of the obligations present in levirate marriage and the binding nature of those obligations is absent from Ruth. Furthermore, there is no evidence that levirate marriage applied outside the immediate family. Finally, it is clear that Naomi despairs of any future for Orpah and Ruth in Bethlehem, indicating that a levirate solution was not known to her.

Frederic Bush offers a helpful discussion of the main issues surrounding Ruth and the levirate custom.[39] He shows clearly that Ruth's marriage was not a levirate marriage in the usual sense of a legal obligation, but that there was "an obligation in *custom* for Boaz or the nearer redeemer to marry Ruth. . . . I agree that there was no legal obligation, but I would insist that there was a

33. Manor, "Brief History," 137.
34. Ibid., 133.
35. Ibid., 136.
36. Hubbard, *Ruth,* 51.
37. Anderson, "Marriage of Ruth," 183.
38. This argument is developed in detail in ibid., 179.
39. Bush, "Ruth," 221-43.

customary obligation, which, though voluntary, was an acknowledged family obligation recognized by the community."[40] This is an interesting suggestion; but, if there was a customary obligation, then the near redeemer would have known about it and would not have needed Boaz to tell him. I am convinced, therefore, that the story of Ruth is not an account of an enforced levirate marriage but of an act of redemption. I agree with Eskenazi and Frymer-Kensky that, although the conclusion that Ruth's marriage was a levirate union "has been widely accepted for a long time, it is increasingly difficult to support and is best relinquished."[41] Ruth did not ask Boaz to fulfill the role of a brother-in-law, יָבָם/*yābām*. Instead she asked him to be her redeemer, גֹּאֵל/*gō'ēl*. Boaz was a "redeemer," not a "levir."[42]

If we accept that the book of Ruth is about redemption, then the regulations about redeeming the land in Lev 25:23-25 provide useful details for understanding the context of the book of Ruth:

> The land shall not be sold in perpetuity, for the land is mine. For you are strangers and sojourners with me. And in all the country you possess, you shall allow a redemption of the land. If your brother becomes poor and sells part of his property, then his nearest redeemer shall come and redeem what his brother has sold. (ESV)

If we understand the marriage of Ruth as an act of redemption rather than a levirate marriage, this creates a different problem since in the OT redemption is about property, not marriage. Yet the marriage of Ruth was closely related to the redemption of the land. The redeemer who had prior claim to the land seems to have wanted to redeem the land until he learned that there were implications involving Ruth. When Boaz informed him about Ruth he immediately declined because he did not want to jeopardize his own inheritance.

We know that the near redeemer was motivated by the possibility of acquiring more land, but Boaz gave him additional information that invoked an immediate and unequivocal volte-face on his part. He now insisted that Boaz should buy the land, but why did he change his mind so quickly and without hesitation when Boaz mentioned Ruth, and how did Ruth the Moabite com-

---

40. Ibid., 226.

41. Eskenazi and Frymer-Kensky, *Ruth*, xxxv.

42. However, Irmtraud Fischer argues that the usual levirate terminology is missing because of the irregularities in the book of Ruth, including the involvement of a foreign woman. Nevertheless she argues that Ruth's marriage was levirate and "clearly speaks to the legal idea that finally makes it possible for the widow Ruth to be cared for in the house of a new husband and thus to be integrated into society" ("Book of Ruth as Exegetical Literature," 144).

plicate matters so much that So-and-So immediately withdrew his intention to redeem the land? Many have assumed that Boaz revealed that whoever redeemed the land must also marry Ruth. For a discussion about the text of Ruth 4:5, see the commentary section of this book.

The majority of scholars argue that Boaz drew the unknown redeemer's attention to his obligation to marry Ruth if he redeemed the land. On the other hand, D. R. G. Beattie has offered the alternative hypothesis that Boaz declared that he was marrying Ruth. Since any children of such a union would have a prior claim to the land, the unknown redeemer realized that this would cause serious complications for his own family's inheritance prospects. Beattie describes what he believes took place at the city gate:

> Opening his case in a tone of friendly advice Boaz tells the redeemer that Naomi has sold the field and asks him if he wishes to redeem it. . . .
>
> From the redeemer's point of view it seems that he is being offered a bargain. Naomi is a widow, presumably elderly, with no immediate heirs and the redemption of the field must have seemed equivalent to its purchase, so the redeemer eagerly announces "I will redeem it." Here the audience feels that something has gone wrong but then Boaz springs his surprise, on the reader no less than on the redeemer: "I'm going to marry Ruth," he says, "and raise an heir to the field." The prospect is now not so attractive to the redeemer. If he redeems the field he will not own it but will have to put it at the disposal of the son of Boaz and Ruth — whether at the price he paid or without charge is not clear but this is immaterial — there is no profit in it for him and so he announces that he cannot afford the redemption after all. The audience gives a sigh of relief, Boaz redeems the field and marries Ruth, and the story ends happily.[43]

The majority of scholars oppose this solution, arguing that Boaz told the redeemer, "you must marry Ruth." This conclusion is based on the argument that at the threshing floor Boaz linked the two transactions together — the marriage of Ruth and the purchase of the land (3:11-13 ESV):

> And now, my daughter, do not fear. I will do for you all that you ask, for all my fellow townsmen know that you are a worthy woman. And now it is true that I am a redeemer. Yet there is a redeemer nearer than I. Remain tonight, and in the morning, if he will redeem you, good; let him do it. But if he is not willing to redeem you, then, as the LORD lives, I will redeem you.

43. D. R. G. Beattie, "Book of Ruth as Evidence," 266.

In this passage it is clearly not just the land that is being redeemed but also Ruth. While customs about redemption in the Pentateuch do not link marriage and redemption of land, this is what is happening in the book of Ruth. Indeed, Boaz does not speak about redeeming the land but about redeeming Ruth. However, there is ambiguity in his speech, and he perhaps kept his true intentions to himself. His declaration "I will marry Ruth" had to be kept secret from everyone, including the readers, until he could spring the trap and surprise the other redeemer and those listening. Boaz was not Ruth's guardian, and he did not have authority to decide who her future husband could be. Therefore it makes more sense for him to reveal his intention to marry Ruth rather than to uncover some unknown obligation that the other redeemer must keep and risk the possibility that he would be willing to accept.

In conclusion, the legal implications of Ruth's marriage are shrouded in mystery. Beattie made an excellent attempt to obviate the problem, and a growing number of scholars, including Sasson, Green, Holmstedt, Nielsen, Linafelt, and Fewell and Gunn, recognize that, although this approach is not without its problems, it is less problematic than the alternative. Fewell and Gunn explain their reason for following the consonantal text (Ketib) as follows:

> For various reasons we prefer to follow the consonantal text and translate, "The day you acquire the field . . . I acquire Ruth." Reading the text this way maintains the distinction between the laws of redemption and levirate marriage in accordance with the laws in Leviticus and Deuteronomy. This reading also provides an important logical requirement of the plot. A piece of unexpected news causes the near redeemer to back out of his commitment to acquire the field under the obligations of redemption. That news is Boaz's announcement of his marriage "in order to raise up the name of the dead to his inheritance." In other words, the near redeemer is suddenly confronted with the possibility that there could be a male heir to Mahlon and that the land for which he was about to expend good money could eventually revert to that heir.[44]

Moreover, the acceptance of the reading "I acquire Ruth" removes any suggestion that Ruth was just an expendable pawn in a man's game, whose future marriage was determined by others. If Boaz was indeed offering Ruth to the other redeemer as his wife, then he put her future in jeopardy and offered her to another man whom she had never met. This scenario seems to

---

44. Danna Fewell and David M. Gunn, "Boaz, Pillar of Society," 52.

conflict with the overall story and atmosphere of the book of Ruth. Therefore, I tentatively agree with those who suggest that Boaz's message that changed the mind of the other redeemer was not "You must marry Ruth" but "I have decided to marry Ruth."

Character Studies

One of the most interesting ways to approach the book of Ruth is through a study of its characters. Excellent work has been done in this area by Kristen Moen Saxegaard. She makes helpful comments about classifying characters and shows how the classification suggested by Adele Berlin can be used to clarify characterization in the book of Ruth. Characters may be classified as "agent", "type," and "full-fledged character."[45] According to this classification, the term "type" refers to a character who has no real impact on the story and who produces no surprises. This is similar to E. M. Forster's "flat character." "Agents" are characters who are important in the narrative because of the function that they fulfill. Full-fledged or round characters are those who are described in detail and we know more about them. Saxegaard argues that "Naomi and Boaz are clearly full-fledged characters, while Elimelech, Chilion, Mahlon, Orpah, So-and-So and Obed are clearly agents."[46] She points out that these minor characters are "hardly present" in the narrative.

> Elimelech, Mahlon and Chilion die; Orpah turns back; Mr So-and-so backs out; and Obed does not arrive until the last scene. This modest presence of the characters makes them one-dimensional and flat. They do not develop, change or surprise.[47]

On the other hand, she finds the character of Ruth more difficult to classify and suggests that she "may have traits of the 'type' but may also be a full-fledged character."[48]

The significance of these character studies lies in the way that the message of the book of Ruth is conveyed through the personalities, demeanor, and interaction of its characters. The importance of the characters in a narrative is explained clearly by Shimon Bar-Efrat.

45. Berlin, *Character Complexity,* 17.
46. Ibid.
47. Ibid., 73.
48. Ibid., 18.

Their personalities and histories attract the reader's attention to a greater extent than do other components of the narrative (explanations, settings, etc.). They generally arouse considerable emotional involvement; we feel what they feel, rejoice in their gladness, grieve at their sorrow and participate in their fate and experiences. Sometimes the characters arouse our sympathy, sometimes our revulsion, but we are never indifferent to them. We want to know them, to see how they act within their environment, and to understand their motives and desires. We follow their struggles to fulfil their aspirations and pay particular attention to everything they say, for when they speak to one another they are also addressing us.[49]

Therefore, an appraisal of the theological message of the book of Ruth involves a careful study of its characters. A study of the characters, however, highlights the different approaches of scholars to the book of Ruth. Traditionally the characters have been approached as examples of exemplary behavior with transparent motives. More recently, this approach has been challenged. For example, Linafelt expresses the following reservations about the traditional approach.

With regard to the human characters and their motivations, . . . I find that far from exemplifying a simple godliness and unquestioned morality, they are a mass of conflicting desires and vested interests, each of them existing within the bounds of a societal structure that limits a person in severe ways depending on one's gender, social class, and nationality, yet each struggling in some way to transcend or subvert those bounds.[50]

The following study of characters shows awareness of various views, but the primary aim is to interpret the text without reading too much between the lines. "It is tempting", as Saxegaard points out, "to turn the characters into our own inventions, and perhaps make them different from how they were created."[51] The text is frequently ambiguous about the motivation of the characters, and probably deliberately so. Therefore, we shall explore the possible implications of the text in all its complexity without pretending that we can psychoanalyze the characters.

49. Shimon Bar-Efrat, *Narrative Art,* 47.
50. Linafelt, "Ruth," xiv-xv.
51. Saxegaard, *Character Complexity,* 16.

Elimelech

One of the most interesting aspects of this character is his name. It could be translated "God is king" or "My God is king." Commentators vary on the significance that they attach to this name. Some see it as important that the book begins with the death of a character whose name represents the ideal theocratic political emphasis of the period of the judges. As Linafelt observes, Elimelech's name declares "the rule of God rather than a human king."[52] However, we must not suggest that the monarchy denied the role of God as the nation's king. King David did not deny that "God was king," and he showed the possibility of having a human king while at the same time recognizing the ultimate authority of YHWH (1 Kgs 2:1-4).

Apart from his name and his journey to Moab, we know very little about Elimelech. We can deduce that he was wealthy enough to own land in Bethlehem and broadminded enough to emigrate to the neighboring country of Moab during a famine. Elimelech's journey to Moab is mentioned without comment in the book of Ruth, and he is not censored or condemned for making this decision. Readers are left to make their own judgments. Some modern scholars are highly critical of Elimelech's decision to leave Bethlehem. Thus André LaCocque describes Elimelech's "defection" to Moab as "shocking."[53] However, the strongest criticism of Elimelech comes from Jewish sources; in particular the Jewish Midrash is unequivocal in its outright condemnation of Elimelech. It is interesting that in order to back up its criticism the Midrash embellishes the story considerably. According to the Midrash, Elimelech was a very wealthy man who had enough reserves to feed the entire population of the land for ten years. When the famine came, he fled so that he could avoid supplying the needs of others.[54] From this perspective, his death in Moab was divine judgment.

However, this is not where the book of Ruth places its emphasis. Elimelech is a character who provides a context for the story but has no main part to play. Saxegaard draws attention to the way in which the narrative quickly dismisses Elimelech when it refers to him as "Naomi's husband" (Ruth 1:3).[55] In this way the text moves the attention away from Elimelech and onto Naomi. The emphasis is on Naomi returning to Bethlehem, not on Elimelech leaving there. This is why we are given so much detail about Naomi and so little about Elimelech.

52. Linafelt, "Ruth," 3.
53. LaCocque, *Ruth*, 39.
54. Rabinowitz, *Midrash Rabbah: Ruth*, 1:4 (pp. 20-21).
55. Saxegaard comments, "Identifying a man by his wife's name is exceptional" (*Character Complexity*, 63).

Orpah

Orpah was married to Kilion. She and Ruth suffered widowhood and were faced with an uncertain future. Nothing negative is said about Orpah in the book. Her return to her mother's house was encouraged by Naomi, and, in the circumstances, it seemed the most obvious thing to do.

However, as Phyllis Trible observes, although Orpah was given advice by Naomi and followed that advice, to return home was her personal decision. She appears in the story as "a whole human being, one who chooses her destiny."[56]

Interpreters both ancient and modern have been particularly unkind to her. Even the identification of her name as linked to the Hebrew word עֹרֶף/'ōrep, "neck," is negative. Some argue that the name Orpah is linked to her action in turning her neck away from her mother-in-law. However, there is no suggestion of this in the text. Jewish sources embellish the story with an account of how she was raped on the return journey to her home. All of this misses the point that the text does not make a judgment on her character, and her return home simply removes her from the story. The main role that Orpah plays in the story is to show that she did what was expected and sensible, which highlights the decision that Ruth makes as extraordinary and totally selfless.

Ruth

Ruth is the sixth person who is introduced in the book that bears her name. Elimelech, Naomi, Mahlon, Kilion, and Orpah are all mentioned before her. She was married to Mahlon, the firstborn of Elimelech and Naomi, but became a widow while still relatively young. Together with Orpah, she was praised by Naomi for her loyalty to her husband, but she was expected to return with Orpah to her home and her own gods. Ruth refused to do this. Her decision seems inexplicable. No divine vision encouraged her, and Naomi did all she could to discourage her.

Ruth's strong character is shown in her insistence to stay with Naomi and also in Naomi's realization that there was no point in arguing with Ruth. Although Athalya Brenner thinks that "Ruth has a contract implying that she has to work for Naomi, she has to take care of the older woman,"[57] one could argue that the opposite is the case. Naomi's attempt to return alone probably reflects her fear that she will need to care for the younger woman. She did not see Ruth

---

56. Trible, *God and Rhetoric*, 171.
57. Athalya Brenner, "Ruth as a Foreign Worker," 159.

as her potential caregiver but as a vulnerable foreign woman who would need continual help. Naomi did not propose that Ruth should go out and glean; it was Ruth's initiative. It is clear that the person whom Naomi originally saw as a burden became a blessing.

Boaz's speech of appreciation highlighted the sacrifice that Ruth had made. Boaz's words are reminiscent of Abraham's call to leave his homeland. However, Trible argues convincingly that Ruth had not only shown faith like Abraham but had also shown superior faith, since when Abraham set out for Canaan he already had substantial security with a wife and an entourage of servants and possessions. Furthermore, Abraham had a clear call from God and divine promises and assurances that were not available to the young widow from Moab.

> Ruth stands alone; she possesses nothing; no God has called her; no deity has promised her blessing; no human being has come to her aid. She lives and chooses without a support group, and she knows that the fruit of her decision may well be the emptiness of rejection, indeed of death. Consequently, not even Abraham's leap of faith surpasses this decision of Ruth's.[58]

Naomi also pointed out the folly of the decision that Ruth was taking. Common sense, given the structure of that society, dictated that Ruth should be searching for a husband and not teaming up with another woman who could offer no prospects of a future bridegroom. Thus Ruth made her decision without any illusion about the enormity of what she was doing.[59]

Ruth was described by Boaz as a "strong woman" or "virtuous woman," אֵשֶׁת חַיִל/'ēšet ḥayil (3:11). Bledstein suggests that in this story the term means "a woman of sound judgment, wholesome values, and energetic pursuit of what is important."[60] This strength of character is reflected in Ruth's approach to Boaz. When Naomi sent her to the threshing floor at night, Naomi assumed that Boaz would tell Ruth what to do, but it happened the other way around: Ruth told Boaz what she wanted him to do for both of them.

Normal language in that society was that the man would "take" the woman to be his wife, but as Fischer points out,

> Ruth is accepted as the active one, even by the elders and the whole people. According to them she is not being "taken" by Boaz, as getting married is

---

58. Trible, *God and Rhetoric*, 173.

59. Trible comments that "a young woman has committed herself to the life of a old woman rather than to the search for a husband, and she has made this commitment not 'until death us do part' but beyond death" (ibid.).

60. Adrien J. Bledstein, "Female Companionships," 124.

usually called in male speech. Ruth "comes" (4.11, בוא) — independently
and on her own initiative — to the house of Boaz.[61]

Thus throughout the book the strength and assertiveness of Ruth are
prominent. As Madipoane J. Masenya observes,

> Even though the relationship between Naomi and Ruth is that of a mother
> and daughter, Ruth does not always act according to the advice or instruc-
> tion of the elderly woman: she decides to return with Naomi despite the
> fact that she has been advised otherwise; she tells Boaz what to do despite
> the fact that she has been advised to listen to what Boaz has to say (3:9).[62]

On the other hand, Ruth's assertiveness must be seen in the context of her
loyalty and humility. She always remembered that she was the foreigner and
the handmaiden (2:10).

Following the marriage proposal, Ruth is compared to Rachel, Leah, and
Tamar (4:11-12). As Brenner observes, this could be taken two ways. On the
one hand, it seems to confirm that Ruth is now part of the Israelite family tree
and is no longer the foreigner from Moab. However, Brenner observes that
the reference to these particular ancestresses has a sting since none of them is
regarded as exemplary.[63]

Bonnie Honig comments that the contrast between Ruth and Orpah
suggests that "Ruth's migration to Bethlehem does not mean that Israel is
now a borderless community open to all foreigners, including even idolatrous
Moabites. Israel is open to the Moabite who is exceptionally virtuous, to Ruth
but not Orpah."[64]

Honig argues that it is significant that the story ends with the baby on
Naomi's lap (4:16), and she suggests that when "Naomi takes Obed from Ruth,
that signals the community's continuing fear of Ruth's foreignness. Ruth the
Moabite cannot be trusted to raise her son properly, in the Israelite way."[65] The
book of Ruth is making clear that Ruth is now fully integrated into Israelite
society and her son is raised as an Israelite. Any danger of Moabite traditions
being assimilated into Israelite society is guarded against by the role played by
Naomi and her community.

Brenner draws attention to the way in which Ruth becomes virtually "in-

---

61. Fischer, "Book of Ruth: 'Feminist' Commentary?" 32.
62. Masenya, "Ngwetši (Bride)," 90.
63. Brenner, "Ruth as a Foreign Worker," 161.
64. Bonnie Honig, "Ruth, the Model Emigrée," 55-56.
65. Ibid., 60.

visible" at the end of "her" story. Although there are many ways to interpret this feature of the story, Brenner suggests that one possible approach is to compare Ruth's fate with that of young immigrant female workers in Israel today. She suggests that Ruth could be understood as "a prime example" of "a low-class foreign woman, a worker without property," who will be "*absorbed* rather than *integrated*" into the host community.[66] This is an interesting comparison and highlights the issues facing foreign workers today, but from the standpoint of the book of Ruth the invisibility at the end of the book is compensated for by the title of the work, which does not allow us to forget that this is Ruth's story.

In conclusion, the overall impression we get about Ruth is that she was strong and assertive. Her role in the book takes many twists and turns, and her innermost thoughts and motives are never entirely clear; but no one could doubt her total commitment to Naomi and her brave determination to succeed.

Naomi

As Adele Berlin points out, "Naomi is the central character in the book," and "all other characters stand in relation to her."[67] This statement may seem surprising since the title of the book leads us to think that Ruth is the main character. However, everything that Ruth does is for Naomi's sake. We have much clearer insights into Naomi's situation than that of anyone else. It is Naomi who lost her husband and two children and who then held Shaddai responsible. It is Naomi who returned to Bethlehem accompanied by Ruth. The marriage to Boaz was orchestrated by Naomi, and when the baby was born the women of Bethlehem said, "A son has been born to Naomi" (4:17 ESV). Naomi is not only the central character of the book but also the person who experienced the greatest personal transformation. This can be seen not only in her change from bitterness to blessing and from emptiness to fulfillment but also in her attitude to men and women. Throughout the story, Naomi values men more than women and cannot conceive of fulfillment without a husband and sons. However, the book concludes with the observation that the Moabite Ruth is worth more than seven sons (4:15).

The catalogue of disasters that befell Naomi is related succinctly. Like Job, she faced one tragedy after another, and also like Job these tragedies were not portrayed as punishment for sin. Although there are fundamental differences between the message of the book of Ruth and the book of Job (discussed be-

66. Brenner, "Ruth as a Foreign Worker," 162.
67. Adele Berlin, *Poetics*, 83.

low), both books show that attempts to find a theological explanation for every tragedy are unhelpful. In the book of Job, no explanation is given to him for his suffering, and it is made clear that it was not punishment. Job's friends wanted him to play the part of a guilty person, but he refused since he knew that he had not done anything to deserve the tragedies that befell him.

Nevertheless, Naomi must have regretted the decision to move to Moab and perhaps even felt guilty that they had made that decision. At least this is how many people have understood the story, and it is also an approach of many modern readers. Although the book itself remains silent about the rights and wrongs of going to Moab, the readers would come to this book with their own prejudices. Furthermore, as Danna Fewell and David Gunn have shown in their imaginative retelling of the story, it is probable that Naomi would at least have considered the possibility that they should never have left Bethlehem: "Naomi was just getting used to living in Moab, when Elimelech dropped down dead. Just like that. No reason. Naomi was devastated. She also felt angry. She knew they shouldn't have come."[68] Of course, Fewell and Gunn know that in trying to get under the skin of the characters, they are attempting the impossible. Nevertheless, it is reasonable to assume that Naomi would know the story about how the Moabite women seduced the men of Israel and brought God's judgment at Baal-peor (Num 25:1-9). Even if she was a very free thinker who sought to rise above racial prejudice, it is highly probable that all the tragedies would cause doubts to arise about whether they were being punished because they had left the promised land.

From the standpoint of modern family life, we can envisage Naomi and Elimelech enjoying a quiet evening together and discussing the situation in Bethlehem. Together they consider the options and agree that there is no future in Bethlehem and that the journey to Moab would be preferable to the much longer journey to Egypt. Thus we can imagine them agreeing to leave their land behind and head for Moab. However, in the patriarchal setting of the book of Ruth, this joint decision-making would have been unlikely. It is possible, if not probable, that Naomi would not have been consulted regarding the move to Moab. There is, for example, no indication that Abraham consulted Sarah before leaving for Canaan, and even his willingness to offer up their son as a sacrifice to have been his decision alone. Was this why Naomi felt that God had dealt harshly with her? Did she feel that she was being punished for a decision that someone else made? This is how Fewell and Gunn reconstruct the opening scene of the book: "Elimelech did not ask her if she wanted to move to Moab. In fact Naomi had some real reservations about going to live among

68. Fewell and Gunn, *Compromising Redemption*, 25.

those heathens. Moab, the children of Lot, a people born of incest, that's what she'd always heard."[69]

Although this imaginative reconstruction of Naomi's innermost thoughts is interesting and may be correct, the book of Ruth itself does not reveal exactly what Naomi was thinking, and there is considerable ambiguity about the character of Naomi. The paucity of information about Naomi's true feelings has left room for scholars to portray Naomi in completely different ways. One of the most sympathetic treatments is that of Trible, who views Naomi as a "model of selflessness, her dominant concern being for the welfare of her daughters-in-law."[70] According to Trible, Naomi's speech to Orpah and Ruth suggests that her "counsel is customary, her motive altruistic, and her theology tinged with irony."[71] However, Fewell and Gunn draw attention to Naomi's strange reaction following Ruth's famous speech: that reaction was one of silence — "And when Naomi saw that she was determined to go with her, she said no more" (1:18 ESV). This silence is sometimes interpreted as indicating merely that she "ceased to argue the point."[72] However, this silence continues when they arrive at Bethlehem, since Naomi's address to the women of the town does not even mention her companion (1:20-21). Perhaps this suggests that Naomi was not overjoyed by Ruth's presence with her. Was Ruth a reminder of past experiences that Naomi would have preferred to forget, and was it embarrassing for her to arrive in Bethlehem with a Moabitess as her only companion? Perhaps Naomi was unsure how the people of Bethlehem would react to the presence of a woman from Moab. Naomi herself had learned to set aside her ethnic prejudices, but she could not be sure whether Ruth would receive a welcome in the parochial setting of Bethlehem.

At the beginning of the story, Naomi's future was uncertain, and she felt miserable and forsaken. Even her faith in God did nothing to ease her sense of deprivation, because she felt that even he had forsaken her. It was difficult to shake herself out of this sense of misery, and it is not surprising in those circumstances that her first thought was not about either the daughter-in-law who had gone home or the one who had accompanied her against her will. It did not occur to her that the Moabite woman whose company she had not wanted would be the source of relief and future hope that she so much longed for.[73] However, it is also clear that after they settled in Bethlehem Ruth's faith-

69. Ibid.

70. Fewell and Gunn, "Son Is Born to Naomi," 99.

71. Trible, *God and Rhetoric*, 171.

72. Peter W. Coxon, "Was Naomi a Scold?" 25.

73. For further insights regarding the relationship of Naomi to her daughters-in-law, see Fewell and Gunn, "Son Is Born to Naomi," 99-100.

fulness to her mother-in-law was well known, and Boaz had heard these good reports that could only have come from Naomi. Any resentment that Naomi had about Ruth's decision to accompany her probably soon dissipated when they arrived in Bethlehem.

After the arrival in Bethlehem, the focus of the book is not on Naomi but on Ruth. She takes the initiative to glean, and the activity of Naomi is not reported. She had no influence on where Ruth should glean, and she did not share details about the identity of Boaz until Ruth mentioned him first. Naomi had both knowledge and contacts in Bethlehem, but she apparently did not inform Ruth about them and made no effort to contact anyone. She appeared to be waiting for others to take the initiative.

However, the turning point for Naomi from bitterness to hope arrived when Ruth related that she had been working in the field of Boaz. Then Naomi exclaimed,

> "May he be blessed by the LORD, whose kindness has not forsaken the living or the dead!" Naomi also said to her, "The man is a close relative of ours, one of our redeemers." (2:20 ESV)

It is possible grammatically that the reference to the one "whose kindness has not forsaken the living or the dead" could refer to either Boaz or YHWH. However, in the commentary above I have argued that the reference is to YHWH, not to Boaz. The remarkable thing from Naomi's point of view was that without prior planning Ruth had found herself in the field of a person who could help them and deliver them from poverty. Naomi's exclamation shows that she did not regard Ruth's choice of field as "good luck" but as a sign that in spite of her earlier bitterness against God, he was working on their behalf. She mentioned the dead because Boaz was not just a wealthy man but also well placed to "redeem" the land that had once provided an income to her husband, Elimelech.

The next initiative in the story is taken by Naomi herself. Any hopes that she once held about the relationship between Boaz and Ruth developing into something more formal and lasting had not materialized. Her initiative was full of risk, particularly for Ruth. It was an initiative born out of desperation, and she is neither praised nor condemned in the text for her audacious plan. As in the stories of Tamar/Judah (Gen 38) and Deborah/Barak (Judg 4–5), a woman needed to take the initiative to encourage a man to take action. Some aspects of her plan seem devious, especially her instruction to Ruth to virtually stalk Boaz until he had eaten, drunk, and fallen asleep. A desperate situation required desperate measures. However, the theological significance of Naomi's actions is not easy to assess. Were these desperate measures taken only on her personal initiative or was she acting in faith? Did YHWH play any part in the drama or was this purely a story of human daring? Does the narrator approve of what she did? If so, are her devious methods approved simply because everything worked out well in the end? As Hubbard points out, Naomi's scheme raises important questions:

> The important question, however, is how the author viewed this scheme theologically. Is Naomi portrayed with approval, disapproval, or indifference? Does her plan reflect admirable faith, deplorable unbelief, or nothing significant at all?[74]

Hubbard is very positive about Naomi's scheme, and he argues that "the writer apparently viewed the approach to Boaz as at least appropriate if not necessary." He also suggests that "there are slight indications that the author at least sympathized with Naomi's ploy," and he gives the following reasons:

> The story-teller apparently tells the tale with great pleasure. Witness the playful use of sexually suggestive language, the impersonal description of the characters ("the man," "the woman"), and the sudden emergence of the other kinsman as a complication (v. 12). Further, the later praise of the neighbours (4:14) implies divine approval of the scheme and undoubtedly voices the author's own interpretation of the events leading to Obed's birth. In sum, the writer apparently viewed the approach to Boaz as at least appropriate if not necessary.[75]

Hubbard concludes that Naomi's "role is both as responder to divine initiative and as advancer of its plans."[76]

However, Charles Baylis is critical of Naomi's initiative, which he regards as contrary to Mosaic law.[77] According to Baylis, Naomi should have sent Ruth not to the threshing floor at night but to the city gate in daylight hours. Furthermore, she should have sent her as a widow dressed in mourning clothes and she should not have taken advantage of a man when he was under the influence of food and drink. According to Baylis, Naomi "sought to fulfill natural needs through natural means."[78]

This critical approach to Naomi's initiative has much to commend it.

74. Hubbard, "Naomi's Shrewdness," 289-90.
75. Ibid., 290.
76. Ibid., 290-91.
77. Charles P. Baylis, "Naomi," 429.
78. Ibid., 431.

Just because this is a story in the Bible we should not fail to recognize that what Naomi did was not only full of risk but also wrong. She put Ruth at risk and left the decision about what should happen on the threshing floor to Boaz. Note that the instructions that Naomi gave Ruth took the initiative out of Ruth's hand and gave it to a half-awake Boaz. The narrator gives us a hint of how irregular Naomi's plan was by recording the words of Boaz when he presumably said to himself, "Let it not be known that the woman came to the threshing floor" (3:14 ESV). This statement shows that he was worried that others might find out what had happened and jump to wrong conclusions. Whatever we think of Naomi's initiative, it is clear that this is not the way that Boaz would have done things.

Although the nocturnal events of chapter 4 are recorded without any mention of divine involvement, this is part of the message of the book that the human characters and all their actions are included within a framework of divine providential care. It was YHWH who gave his people food, and this encouraged Naomi to return home; and at the end of the story it is YHWH who enabled Ruth to conceive (4:13). All the human activity proceeds without mentioning YHWH's involvement, but in the end his overall providential care is evident in his performance of the tasks that were outside human control.

Boaz

Scholars have failed to agree on an etymology for the name Boaz. The name at least at a popular level may have been linked to the concept of strength ("In him is strength"; cf. Ps 21:1). One of the pillars of the temple was called "Boaz," and this has given rise to the interesting hypothesis that Solomon named the pillar in honor of Boaz. This theory, while not impossible, has not gained widespread support because of lack of evidence.

Most attempts to understand the role of Boaz portray him in a positive light, but many draw attention to his failure to act until he was forced to do so. Trible shows that although Boaz was wealthy and a man of standing, he did not take the initiative. He admitted that he knew Naomi and that he had heard all that Ruth had done, but he did not take decisive action or offer long-term help until Ruth arrived unannounced in his field. Thus it was Ruth the foreign woman who took the initiative. As Trible observes, "This powerful male has not rushed to the rescue of a destitute female. His graciousness has not sought her out."[79] Although Boaz is the hero and redeemer of the book, his failure to

---

79. Trible, *God and Rhetoric*, 178.

act serves to show the importance of the initiatives of Ruth and Naomi. These women provided the impetus for Boaz to act; without the catalyst of their determined efforts, he would not have acted. The Hebrew text of the book conveys something of his inner nervousness when he encounters Ruth at midnight on the threshing floor. According to Linafelt, "When Ruth appears next to Boaz in the middle of the night in chapter 3, he is clearly flustered, more than a little frightened, and acquiesces to her suggestions quite easily."[80] This suggests that Boaz's failure to act may be understood as a lack of confidence and a nervousness about the future. He may also have been reticent to promote his own interests since he was not the closest relative.

However, some scholars judge him much more harshly. Jon Berquist describes Boaz as a "trickster." According to this view, Boaz saw a great opportunity to acquire "Elimelech's property at cost." However, he was prevented from doing so because another relative had a prior claim to the land. Thus, according to Berquist, the decision of Boaz to marry Ruth was "a perfect plan to maximize his own wealth, if only he can trick his relative out of his rights to redeem the property."[81]

Berquist is not the only one who sees Boaz in a negative light. Fewell and Gunn take a similar approach. They question the motives of Boaz and draw attention to his protectiveness of Ruth reflected in his desire that she stay with the women and keep away from the men. They suggest that he was motivated by the desire to marry Ruth rather than by the desire to provide for his relative Naomi. As mentioned above, Boaz's reluctance to take the initiative is often explained in the context of his knowledge that the initiative lay with the closer kinsman. However, Fewell and Gunn argue that Boaz, as a pillar of society, "cannot afford to pursue his interest in a Moabite woman, unless under some kind of cloak or compulsion."[82] Naomi provides the compulsion because she knows exactly what is preventing him from acting.

Although most scholars praise the tact and skill that Boaz uses in his confrontation with the other redeemer, Fewell and Gunn suggest that it was deliberately orchestrated by Boaz to give him credit and to provide a good excuse for marrying a Moabite woman:

> Why the public confrontation? Because the essence of Boaz's operation here is public. He is in the business of effecting a dubious marriage in such a way as to make it a public triumph. He is a pillar of society and determined to

80. Linafelt, "Ruth," xv.
81. Berquist, "Role Differentiation," 34.
82. Fewell and Gunn, "Boaz, Pillar of Society," 49.

remain that way. The name of the game is PR and he is a master of it. The redeemer, therefore, is the luckless victim of a setup. . . . Why confrontation? Because that way Boaz comes out a winner and people love a winner.[83]

In the introduction to this commentary, I referred to the recurring ambiguity in the book of Ruth. The possibility of understanding Boaz in different ways is one aspect of that ambiguity. In the final analysis, Boaz appears as a very human figure, who genuinely wants the best for others but whose failure of nerve forced the women to take serious risks to gain his attention. However, the book offers us no insight into the motives of the characters in the book of Ruth, but it takes us on a journey to the final denouement in which the birth of a son points forward to Israel's greatest king. The characters operate within the framework of their own fears, prejudices, and aspirations, but in conjunction with them and even in spite of them YHWH is working out his own purposes.

The Supervisor

The statement that the supervisor made to Boaz has given rise to a great deal of discussion. How much authority did he have? What did Ruth ask him for? Did he grant her request? Did he allow Ruth to glean or did she stand around all morning waiting for Boaz to come? Why does he mention that Ruth was resting in a shelter/house (2:7)? These questions arise because the text itself is difficult to translate. An understanding of the character of the supervisor depends on how we resolve the ambiguity in the text. (See the discussion of these textual problems in the commentary section.)

It is noteworthy that the supervisor does not approach Boaz with information about Ruth. On the contrary, Boaz approaches the supervisor and asks him about her. This immediately shows the weakness of the suggestion that Ruth has been standing around all morning waiting for permission that the supervisor could not grant (this view is discussed in the commentary above). If this had been the case we should have expected the supervisor to have approached Boaz rather than the other way around. But why does Boaz ask, "Whose young woman is this?" What drew his attention to Ruth? In the commentary, I have suggested that perhaps she was the one person in the field who did not know the identity and status of this man who had arrived from Bethlehem. All the others knew that he was the boss and acted accordingly. Ruth did not know who he was and continued to enjoy a short break, thus

---

83. Ibid., 52.

unwittingly drawing attention to herself. Boaz is not used to seeing someone having an unofficial break, and he challenges the supervisor about her identity. In answer to Boaz's question, the supervisor makes two things clear. First, this woman is here to glean, she has not been employed; and second, the rest that she is having is well deserved.

The foreman's reply to Boaz does suggest that he was very defensive, but it is not clear why this should be. An interesting possibility is suggested by Jonathan Grossman. He suggests that the "boy" (Grossman's term) is suspicious of Ruth and that he was alarmed that she was gathering so much grain.[84] Perhaps the boy was worried that he might be reprimanded by Boaz for allowing Ruth to glean, especially since she had done very well and accumulated more grain than he had expected when he gave her permission. He was therefore making excuses for both himself and Ruth.

Another approach is suggested if we take the term "house" seriously. According to the Hebrew text the supervisor refers to a short rest in the "house." Most translations interpret this as a shelter for the workers. However, what happens if we understand this as the house of Boaz? Berquist reconstructs the scene: "Boaz entered his property and passed by the field workers on the way to his house, where a surprise awaited him: his field supervisor with a foreign woman. With apt suspicion, Boaz challenged the supervisor, 'Who is this woman?' "[85] If Boaz was suspicious about what was happening between his supervisor and Ruth, his warning that she should stay with his women makes perfect sense. However, it is very unlikely that Boaz had built a house in the countryside. He arrived from Bethlehem, and it is probably in the town itself that he owned a house. But if we accept that a shelter is referred to, it is possible that Boaz found his supervisor with a woman in the workers' shelter and this raised his suspicions, which in the end were unfounded.

We should also note that the supervisor's description of Ruth emphasizes her foreignness. In his short description of her he does not use a personal name but mentions her foreign origins twice — she is a Moabite woman from Moab.

Since the supervisor is not a main character in the story, we should probably understand his role as simply to introduce these two main characters. The narrator does not draw attention to the supervisor but uses this minor character to show how Ruth and Boaz met. The supervisor also fulfills the role of emphasizing the foreignness of Ruth. Everywhere she went she was known as the woman who came from Moab.

84. Jonathan Grossman, "Gleaning among the Ears," 703-16.
85. Jon L. Berquist, "Role Dedifferentiation," 29.

So-and-So

The Hebrew expression פְּלֹנִי אַלְמֹנִי/*pĕlōnî ʾalmōnî* refers to the redeemer who had priority over Boaz and had the opportunity to redeem the land of Elimelech. It is not a name but is best translated as "So-and-So." His only contribution was in terms of what he did not do, and he acts as a foil to Boaz.

God

Throughout this book I have drawn attention to the ambiguity in the narrative. The characters themselves are ambiguous, as we have seen; but even more ambiguous is the understanding of the role of God in the narrative. On only one occasion do we read about a direct action of YHWH, and this relates to the conception of Obed (4:13). The only other reference to an action of God in the narrative relates to the comment that Naomi *had heard* that YHWH had visited his people to give them food (1:6). This absence of the activity of God in the book allows readers to decide whether the book suggests underlying divine providence or simply a human story. As Linafelt comments, "one reader's sense of hidden providential workings is another reader's sense of God's absence."[86] Thus the book of Ruth is true to life. Some people will judge what happens to them in the light of their faith in the providence of God, and others will judge daily events as purely coincidence. Just as life leaves us this choice, the book of Ruth leaves the reader to decide. However, the final section of the book, which indicates that God's plans for the Davidic monarchy were being realized through the lives of ordinary people, suggests that this book clearly presupposes that divine providence is at work in the everyday actions of ordinary people.

86. Linafelt, "Ruth," xvi-xvii.

Theological Issues, Themes, and Approaches

Creation, Providence, and Guidance

The doctrine of creation is not mentioned frequently in the OT, but this does not mean that it is unimportant. The doctrine of creation provides a foundation for understanding the relationship between God and the world that he created. Much of what is taught about God is understood in the light of his acts of creation and his status as the creator. Furthermore, creation is closely linked to divine providence. God takes responsibility for his creation and is involved in managing it and controlling it. This providential care operates at different levels. It is seen in God's provision of rain and his control of the elements (Gen 2:5; Deut 11:14; Ps 147:8). At a personal level, God's continued involvement is seen in the experiences of people. This is witnessed in the book of Genesis, but there is also evidence of it in the book of Ruth and indeed throughout the OT (e.g., Gen 12:1-3).

The OT bears witness to a wide range of experience in relation to receiving divine guidance and intervention. In the book of Genesis the communications between God and human beings take place in many different ways involving various degrees of intimacy. The book begins with contrasting and yet complementary accounts of creation. The first account shows God at a distance speaking the universe into being by his powerful words, while the second account describes God actively forming the first human being as a potter would mold a clay vessel.

These contrasting images of God are held in tension in Genesis and provide an interpretive key for understanding the theology not only of Genesis but of the OT as a whole. God, at one and the same time, is the distant, holy God enthroned in the heavens and also the God who is intimately involved in human affairs. Thus in the OT (and in the NT) God is seen from two different perspectives: the heavenly perspective and the perspective that was informed through his encounter with people — the earthly perspective.

In the account of Abraham the divine activity reflects the approach of the second creation account, the earth perspective. We are introduced to God appearing on earth, eating a meal, and sharing with Abraham his deep concerns about the behavior of the cities of Sodom and Gomorrah (Gen 18:1-33). However, in the same narrative cycle the divine activity in relation to the servant of Abraham is much less intimate. Having been given the daunting task of finding a suitable wife for Isaac, the servant recognized his need of guidance and he believed that God would guide him. The servant did not see God and had no verbal communication from God, yet he believed that God was with him and he expected God to show his will through everyday events. He relied on a series of "coincidences" to discern God's will.

> And he said, "O LORD, God of my master Abraham, please grant me success today and show steadfast love to my master Abraham. Behold, I am standing by the spring of water, and the daughters of the men of the city are coming out to draw water. Let the young woman to whom I shall say, 'Please let down your jar that I may drink,' and who shall say, 'Drink, and I will water your camels' — let her be the one whom you have appointed for your servant Isaac. By this I shall know that you have shown steadfast love to my master." (Gen 24:12-14 ESV)

The servant of Abraham experienced the value of a pragmatic faith in the God who he believed was present with him to fulfill the promises that he had made to Abraham. This faith was rewarded in that he received the guidance he required and was blessed with success in his mission.

In the Jacob story both aspects of divine providence come together. God appeared at Bethel, but is he understood as distant from or close to Jacob? Most of our translations suggest distance. The top of the stairway is in heaven, and that is where God is located. However, the Hebrew is ambiguous, and it is possible to understand the passage as meaning that "God stood beside him." This is Jacob's own understanding: "Surely the LORD is in this place; and I knew it not" (28:16 KJV). Although Jacob's experience at Bethel is described as a dream, it is nevertheless a life-changing experience, and the medium of the dream does not lessen the reality or the immediacy of the occasion. Jacob's experience at Peniel is a further example of a close personal encounter with YHWH (32:24-30). Again, the encounter was during the hours of darkness, but this time there is no suggestion that it was a dream. However, from Peniel onward the encounters with God tend to be in dreams and visions. Jacob is reassured during his journey to Egypt by "visions of the night" (46:2).

All Joseph's encounters with God were through dreams, and his contemporaries had similar insights into the divine world. However, nothing approaches the experiences of Abraham or Jacob. It is significant that Joseph's understanding of God came not only through dreams; he was also able to discern the hand of God in history. After his father's death, Joseph reassured his brothers that God was at work in human history, and even their evil deeds had been used by God for the ultimate good of all concerned (50:20).

This insight of Joseph is particularly relevant for the story of Ruth. As Joseph discerned the hand of God in history, the reader of Ruth is encouraged to see that although in many ways there are no close encounters with God in the book of Ruth, the providential care of YHWH is discernible in every turn of events. Thus the role of God in Ruth is very different from Genesis. There are no direct appearances, no visions, and no dreams in Ruth. Katheryn Pfisterer Darr reminds us that

> the sun does not stand still for Ruth; no one is swallowed by a fish. YHWH does not appear as a divine warrior, ensuring Israelite victory over its foes. Rather, God works behind the scenes through characters who triumph over adversity by acts of extraordinary devotion and initiative.[1]

Ruth's determination to turn her back on Moab and accompany Naomi to Bethlehem was not in response to any divine communication; her primary motivation was love. Furthermore, Ruth found herself in Boaz's field, but at first she did not know how crucial this choice would turn out to be; it is even described in the text as a "chance" happening (Ruth 2:3). Similarly, Naomi used her initiative to send Ruth to the threshing floor without any divine directive to do so (3:1-4). Yet the book of Ruth shows that behind all these human initiatives, God was present and active, though the main characters in the drama were not aware of his presence. The overall message of the book is that Naomi, Ruth, and Boaz were all guided and provided for by the unseen and impalpable presence of God. They were under the providential care of God.

Karl Barth defines providence as "the superior dealings of the Creator with his creation, the wisdom, omnipotence and goodness with which He maintains and governs in time this distinct reality according to the counsel of His own will."[2] Barth has argued convincingly that one aspect of God's providential

---

1. Katheryn Pfisterer Darr, *Far More Precious than Jewels*, 59.
2. Karl Barth, *Church Dogmatics*, 3/3:3.

care is what he terms "The Divine Accompanying." According to Barth, the creature accompanied by God may not be aware of the divine presence. The creature acts freely and "goes its own way, but in fact it always finds itself in a very definite sense on God's way."[3] Thus what appeared to be luck or good fortune to Ruth when she entered the field of Boaz was the result of God's providential care and his divine presence working out his plan not only for Ruth and Naomi but also for the future of the people of Israel.

The Hiddenness of God

What makes the book of Ruth so relevant for us is that the experience of the characters, particularly Naomi, is not far removed from the experience of many people today. Naomi felt that God was far away, she found no comfort from him, and her thoughts about God were more confusing than helpful. Her problem was the bitter human predicament of feeling forsaken by God that many people today could identify with; it is not unusual for Christians to pass through difficult periods when God seems far away. However, the message of the book of Ruth is that God's absence was only apparent and he was very much in control and was moving events toward his chosen denouement. God's way of working out his purposes is through people. God chooses people through whom he influences events in the world, even though his presence is sometimes imperceptible.

In the way that it portrays the activity and presence of God, the book of Ruth is reminiscent of the book of Job. In both books the main characters did not understand why they were going through such difficult times. However, Job's relationship with God differed from Naomi's. Job wanted to confront God and challenge him to explain his circumstances, and he addressed God directly (Job 23:3-4). Naomi in weary resignation complained that God had dealt bitterly with her. There are other differences between the message of the book of Job and the book of Ruth. Kristin Saxegaard has highlighted these differences, and she sums up her comparison between Job and Naomi in the following way: "Different from Job, she [Naomi] is not alone. She has Ruth. But also different from Job, she never addresses God, and she does not express any understanding of God at the end of the story."[4] Saxegaard suggests that the silence in the final chapter about how Naomi felt after Ruth's marriage "raises the question of whether Naomi has abandoned God because of her experiencing that God has

3. Ibid., 94.
4. Saxegaard, *Character Complexity*, 104.

abandoned her."[5] The text does not discuss Naomi's relationship with God at the end of the book, while in the book of Job the sufferer's relationship with God is a main focus of the final chapters. Thus we must be careful about drawing too close a comparison between these two books.

A term that is relevant in this context and that has a useful application to the book of Ruth is the "hiddenness of God."[6] A study of the hiddenness of God highlights those occasions in the Bible where people have not been able to understand or comprehend the role of God in a particular situation. It was the hiddenness of God that led to Naomi's complaint since she could not understand why such terrible circumstances had ruined her life. Naomi's sense of alienation from God was echoed by many others in the OT, particularly in the Psalms. In most examples of people who experienced the hiddenness of God, their reaction was to ask questions. As Samuel Balentine observes, "Questions directed toward God are characteristic elements in psalms of lamentation."[7] These questions typically begin with: "Why?" (10:1; 44:24); "How long?" (89:46); "When?" (119:84); "Where?" (89:49). Naomi did ask "why?" but she was addressing the women of Bethlehem, not YHWH. The absence of any prayer or question addressed to God by Naomi emphasizes her sense of Godforsakenness. She had given up trying to understand God's ways, and in this sense her predicament was worse than that of Job.

The bitterness of Job and Naomi conveys an important message since the readers of both books are aware that the bitterness will not last forever. In relation to Job, the readers are aware that although Job is frustrated by the apparent indifference of God to his plight, there is a heavenly dimension to the story that will be unveiled in the denouement of the drama. Similarly, the reader of Naomi's story understands her bitterness in the light of the well-known conclusion to the story since this bitter woman will have her joy restored and will share in the joy and future hope that will be personified by the arrival of Ruth's baby, Obed. The message that these stories convey is that the hiddenness of God is temporary, and when it appears that God is doing nothing in a particular situation, our response should not be despair but faith in God's providence.

The significance of the study of the hiddenness of God in the book of Ruth is that it highlights the truth that the hiddenness of God "is not always and in every case to be understood as a manifestation of divine judgment in response

---

5. Ibid.

6. The concept of the "hiddenness of God" is used by Fredrik Lindström in relation to the individual complaints in the Psalms. See *Suffering and Sin,* 454.

7. Samuel E. Balentine, *Hidden God,* 117.

to man's sinfulness."[8] Often, both in ancient and modern times, people facing difficulties have felt abandoned by God, and their sense of abandonment is not to be understood as judgment for sin. Rather they are simply sharing with Naomi the dark tunnel experience where God's apparent absence makes no sense. Naomi's experience shows that the hiddenness of God should not be understood as the absence of God.

The Theme of Land

This section explores the theological and social implications of Israel's understanding of land as a gift from God. The corollary of the OT understanding of land meant that it highlighted human responsibility toward land to the extent that land could be understood as a spiritual thermometer for testing people's relationship with God and with one another.[9] As Walter Brueggemann comments, the theme of land is used symbolically in the Bible "to express the wholeness of joy and well-being characterized by social coherence and personal ease in prosperity, security, and freedom."[10]

The idea of having a relationship with land may seem inappropriate to many in the modern world: relationships are formed with people and sometimes even with animals, but how can it be said that someone has a relationship with land? Yet this is exactly what happens in the OT, as several scholars have highlighted.[11] In Genesis Adam is formed from the dust of the land, and he has a close relationship with it that may be described as interdependent. Without the human being to till the land, it does not produce its best. However, when Adam fulfills his duty toward the land, it produces food for him (Gen 2:16).

The theme of land in the OT is not only significant in view of its importance for human beings; it also has important theological significance. In connection with the theme of land the imminence and presence of God with his creation is clearly presented in the OT. Any suggestion that God is indifferent to or distant from his creation is dispelled by the description of him planting a garden and making human beings from the soil (Gen 2:5-9). The mention of God walking in the garden in the cool of the day further emphasizes that while he is separate from creation, God is present and actively involved (3:8).

The relationship that humans have with land is indicative of their rela-

---

8. Ibid., v.

9. Walter Brueggemann, *Land*, 2.

10. Ibid.

11. See, e.g., Terence E. Fretheim, *God and World*; Brueggemann, *Land*; C. J. H. Wright, *Living as the People of God*.

tionship with God. It may be described as a tripartite relationship — humans relate to land and they relate to God and these relationships are interrelated. A failure to maintain a close relationship with God could have implications for a person's relationship with the land (Gen 3:17-19). On the other hand, as Isaac discovered, a good relationship with God could enhance the productivity of the land (26:12). The tripartite relationship among God, humans, and land in the garden of Eden portrayed the ideal for which Israel must aim. In Eden God's presence was openly manifest, and there was communion with him (3:8-12).

This understanding of God's relationship with people and their relationship with him and with land is discussed in detail by Terence Fretheim, who argues that "God's relationship with the world is comprehensive in scope." He shows that God's ongoing relationship with his creation means that he is "present on every occasion and active in every event."[12] Yet God's presence does not mean that he micromanages every detail of human life. God created the land but he did not cultivate it (Gen 2:5). Human beings still had their part to play and were responsible to God for their treatment of the gift of land. This background is important for the book of Ruth, which relates a story of human struggle in which God is rarely mentioned.

Throughout the OT there is unequivocal emphasis that since YHWH created the land, he is its ultimate owner. This is highlighted by Norman Habel, whose book on the subject is significantly titled *The Land Is Mine*. The implications of this divine ownership of land are that "the Israelites are ideologically represented as tenants rather than owners of the land they cultivate."[13] Although people might have regarded themselves as owners of a particular portion of land, they were not outright owners and had to observe the right of YHWH to regulate their usage of his land. As Fretheim notes, "the land is an issue of divine right, not human rights, and human beings are to treat it accordingly, as gift, not possession."[14]

A corollary of understanding the land as a gift is that it is indebted the recipients to the giver.[15] This led to rules about the use, sale, and redemption of land (Lev 25–27; see the section below on "Redemption"). Peasants could "sell the use of their land in a crisis and redeem the land in due course."[16]

---

12. Fretheim, *God and World,* 23.

13. Habel, *Land Is Mine,* 98.

14. Fretheim, *God and World,* 139.

15. The implications of this for the Christian church are discussed and developed in the *Jubilee Manifesto.* Michael Schluter and John Ashcroft argue that "we express our love for our Creator by respecting his creation and fulfilling our responsibilities towards him" (23).

16. Habel, *Land Is Mine,* 110.

In order to understand the theological implications of landownership in the OT, it is helpful to examine the regulations in the Pentateuch. Leviticus 25 presents laws and regulations regarding land that can be read in conjunction with the land stories in the book of Genesis. The creation narratives show clearly that all land and its allocation are the remit of the Creator himself. We see this worked out in the accounts of Adam, Noah, Abraham, and Jacob. In Leviticus the same theology of land is presented not in story form but in a legal framework. YHWH's ownership of land and his status as the divine landlord are clearly stated in the verse that introduces the subject of land redemption (Lev 25:23 ESV): "The land shall not be sold in perpetuity, for the land is mine. For you are strangers and sojourners with me."

This understanding of land as divine property elevates land and gives it a status and importance that is difficult for modern people to understand. It is not normal for people to think that the land on which their house is built, or their back garden, belongs to God and that they must treat it appropriately. However, this is indeed the biblical emphasis that provides the context for the biblical laws of redemption. The regulations about land in Leviticus are set in the context of making provision for a family member who had fallen on hard times. It seems irrelevant to us today, but not long ago in Ireland these laws not only would have been relevant but would also have saved many lives. The Irish famine (1845-1850) was caused by an airborne disease that destroyed the potato crop, but, tragic as this was, it should not have led to the death of thousands of people. While there were many contributing factors, it was the regulations relating to land that exacerbated the problems and made the disaster inevitable. Irish families did not own land and needed to rent it from "middle men," who bought the right to sublet the land from landlords, some of whom may never even have set foot on the land but exacted a large income from it. The unjust system meant that even when times were good there was no escape from the poverty trap. However, when famine struck, the peasants faced certain starvation and death with no route to escape since they did not own the land. Many chose the dangerous crossing to the New World rather than stay on land that they still had to pay rent for, even though it was producing nothing. It is interesting that many centuries before the famine in Ireland the issues about landownership were relevant in Israel, and the system outlined in Leviticus was designed to prevent people falling into the poverty trap.

Human responsibility toward land is emphasized throughout the Pentateuch. There were laws to be kept concerning the land, and people had certain responsibilities in relation to caring for it and exercising control over it (Gen 2:15-17). Particularly when the Israelites were blessed with fertile land they were to show concern for those who did not have land. Landless people were vulnerable and powerless and had no "standing ground in the community."[17] As Habel observes, "justice for the landless clearly means that those without power and property should not be exploited."[18] They included "the stranger who sojourns with you" (Lev 19:34 ESV). The generosity toward the stranger should be apparent in the way that commerce was carried out and crops harvested. When buying or selling produce from the land, Israelite weights and measures were to be fair and accurate: "You shall do no wrong in judgment, in measures of length or weight or quantity. You shall have just balances, just weights, a just ephah, and a just hin" (Lev 19:35-36 ESV). This divine dimension of landownership had important implications for Israelite farmers. There were obligations that had to be observed in acknowledgment of God's ownership and oversight of land. As mentioned above in the commentary section, the Israelite harvesters were instructed to leave some of their crops in the fields so that food would be available to the poor and needy who have no land of their own (Deut 24:19-20). They were always to remember that the Lord who made these stipulations was the one who brought them out of their poverty and slavery in Egypt (Lev 19:36). The motivation for this concern for the foreigner was articulated in terms of Israel's obligation to YHWH.[19]

Israel was reminded that their God was not exclusively interested in Israelites and, as Fretheim puts it, they could not "confine God's promising activity to their own precincts."[20] Thus God not only made promises to Abraham and Sarah but also to Hagar and Ishmael (Gen 16:10-11; 21:18). The generosity of Boaz in the book of Ruth shows how this worked in practice. Even though a foreigner, Ruth was permitted to glean in the fields during the time of harvest (Ruth 2). An interesting observation about the privilege of gleaning is made by Michael Schluter, who comments on the dignity that this practice afforded the alien since it provided the needy person with meaningful work. On the other hand, Schluter points out that gleaning "would have been hard work for relatively little return, as indicated in the book of Ruth; so no one could feel that this welfare benefit was a 'soft option.'"[21]

---

17. This is argued clearly by Brueggemann, *Land*, 61.

18. Habel, *Land Is Mine*, 52.

19. Michael Schluter, referring to Lev 19:34, argues that "the alien in this verse, has no automatic right to be loved by the Israelite, nor does the Israelite have an obligation directly to the alien to love him. However, for Israel, there is an obligation to love the alien which is an obligation to Yahweh, because of what Yahweh has done for the Israelite in liberating him from Egypt. He is expected to reflect on Yahweh's behaviour, and in the light of that relationship work out what is appropriate in his relationship with the alien" ("Welfare," 177).

20. Fretheim, *God and World*, 105.

21. Schluter, "Welfare," 179.

However, the regulations about gleaning were part of a much wider obligation to acknowledge the ownership of God in all land dealings. This raises questions about the implication of such responsibility for Christian ethics. The connection is made by Brueggemann:

> Land with Yahweh brings responsibility. The same land that is gift freely given is task sharply put. Landed Israel is under mandate. "Everyone to whom much is given, of him will much be required" (Luke 12:48). Interestingly in Luke 12:41-48, Jesus' saying is precisely in the context of possessions, owners, and stewards. It is a radical idea challenging our usual notions of possessions, for we think much possession makes one immune from caring.[22]

This ethical approach is further developed in the *Jubilee Manifesto,* in which Christopher Wright claims that "the reality of the story of God's engagement with creation predicates an ethic of gratitude and mission." He argues that this is not just an OT issue since the "story of Israel and Yahweh is also our story, for if we are 'in Christ,' then, according to Paul, we are also 'in Abraham' and heirs according to the promise."[23]

Another relevant aspect of the theme of land in the OT relates to leaving land and returning to land. This theme is very prominent in the book of Genesis with its stories of expulsion from land in chapters 3 and 4, whereas chapters 12–50 are about acquiring land. On the one hand, Abraham leaves Ur to go to the land that God promised to show him, and his offspring are promised that they shall inherit that land — the land of Canaan. On the other hand, there is more emphasis in Genesis on leaving Canaan. Abraham's first experience of that land was somewhat marred by the discovery that it was in the grip of a severe famine, an event repeated in the book of Ruth (Gen 12:10; Ruth 1:1). As a result of this disappointment, Abraham left Canaan and settled in Egypt. His journey to Egypt is not condemned; indeed, the emphasis that the famine was "severe" seems to vindicate his decision to leave Canaan. It is true that things go badly wrong in Egypt, but this is related to Abraham's cowardly failure to protect his wife (Gen 12:11-20). In contrast, Isaac is rewarded for not going to Egypt during a famine while his son is blessed as he sets out from Canaan to Paddan-aram (Gen 26:1-5; 28:10-22). The final journey of the elderly Jacob to Egypt is clearly sanctioned by God and accompanied by promises of divine protection and blessing (Gen 46:1-4).

22. Brueggemann, *Land*, 56.
23. Christopher Wright, "Ethical Authority," 68.

Furthermore, throughout Exodus–Deuteronomy, the underlying theme is movement toward and preparation to enter the land that God had promised to his people. There are continually echoes of the part that land played in the tripartite relationship among people, land, and God. The land was a place of harmony, freedom, and rest for Israel. However, the threat of expulsion was always present if Israel failed to obey God's law. Expulsion from the land would lead to "no repose," "no resting place for the sole of your foot," "an anxious mind, eyes weary with longing, and a despairing heart" (Deut 28:65 NIV).

As Brueggemann notes, "Israel's faith is essentially a journeying in and out of land, and its faith can be organized around these focuses."[24] The clear land motif that Brueggemann discerns is that "grasping for home leads to homelessness and risking homelessness yields the gift of home."[25] This is a very appropriate way of summarizing an important aspect of the message of the book of Ruth. It is about a Moabite woman who risked homelessness and found her true home.

The Land of Moab

In a speech on the Middle East in 1994, President Clinton referred to Moab as "the land where Moses died and Ruth was born."[26] When we approach the book of Ruth we cannot ignore the part that the land of Moab plays in the story. It is, of course, just the name of a place — the place that Elimelech and Naomi go to and the place that Ruth comes from. However, it is much more than just a location near Bethlehem. It has a history that would have been well known to the readers of the book of Ruth. Before we can fully understand the book of Ruth, we need to put it in the context of the relationship between the Moabites and Israelites.

This relationship began well; the father of the Moabites, Lot, was Abraham's nephew.[27] Lot accompanied Abraham when he left Haran for Canaan. However, in this relationship, Lot always lived in Abraham's shadow. He arrived in Canaan with Abraham, and he traveled to Egypt with him during a famine (Gen 12–13). He returned to Canaan with Abraham, greatly enriched but not as much as his uncle. When quarreling broke out, Abraham took the initiative and made a most generous, magnanimous offer to Lot giving him the opportunity

---

24. Brueggemann, *Land*, 13.
25. Ibid., 202.
26. For this information I am indebted to Honig, "Ruth, the Model Emigrée," 55.
27. The contrast between Lot and Ruth is discussed in the commentary section on 1:14-18.

to choose the part of the land that he preferred. Lot did not choose Canaan but looked out to the east, beyond Canaan to the fertile land near Sodom and Gomorrah. So Lot headed east. Once separated from Abraham, Lot's fortunes went quickly downhill and he was taken prisoner. During this account Lot is entirely passive, and he has to be rescued by his uncle (Gen 14).

Lot's inferiority is further highlighted by the comparison made between the hospitality that Abraham offered to his guests and that offered by Lot (Gen 18–19). Even more significant is the way in which the divine visitors approach the two characters. The three heavenly messengers warmly accepted Abraham's hospitality, but the two visitors to Sodom showed a reluctance to accept hospitality from Lot. Lot's rescue was clearly done for Abraham's sake.

The birth of Lot's children was a story of desperation on the part of his daughters (Gen 19). The offspring from their incestuous relationship with their father became the ancestors of Ammon and Moab. There are echoes here of the desperate measures that Tamar took to have offspring by her father-in-law, Judah.

There is no doubt that Abraham outshines Lot in every way. Israel's understanding of the history of Moab suggested that their origins were inferior when compared to Abraham, the heir of such great promises. The character of Lot provides a comic foil for Abraham. He made bad choices. Abraham went where YHWH directed him, but Lot was guided by his own senses. Abraham's seed was provided by God in circumstances that could only be described as miraculous, but Lot's offspring were provided through his daughters' desperate acts.

Therefore in this story of Ruth the tables are turned on Israel. The land that Lot chose is productive, but Abraham's offspring are suffering because their land, far from flowing with milk and honey, is in the grip of a severe famine. Furthermore, the family tree of Israel's greatest king includes a woman from Moab! In the story of Lot and Abraham there is the hint that Lot may become the heir of Abraham, but their separation makes this unlikely. The book of Ruth tells this story in reverse: Ruth refuses to separate from Naomi and allows devotion to and love for her mother-in-law to be the deciding factor in her choice. Lot left Abraham because he was enticed by the appearance of the land in the east, but things turned out worse than he could have imagined. Ruth, on the other hand, left the land in the east and headed west with Naomi. Ruth was blessed beyond her highest hopes. Lot lost the opportunity, but Ruth seized it tenaciously.

The relationship between Israel and Moab is further highlighted in the story about the attempt of King Balak of Moab to have Israel cursed by Baalam the prophet (Num 22–24). Balak's motivation was fear. According to the Song of Moses, the leaders of Moab trembled when Israel left Egypt (Exod 15:15). The cursing of Baalam did not succeed, but his advice to seduce the Israelites to join a heathen celebration in honor of Baal of Peor brought judgment from YHWH in which twenty-four thousand Israelites lost their lives. A later king of Moab subjugated Israel for eighteen years before being assassinated by Ehud, who then led Israel to a notable victory in which ten thousand Moabites were killed (Judg 3:12-30).

Although Saul's enemies included the Moabites (1 Sam 14:47), David seems to have had a close relationship with Moab before he became king, since he sent his parents there for safety (1 Sam 22:3-4). Later the relations soured, and David treated Moabite prisoners of war with extreme brutality (2 Sam 8:2; this is discussed in more detail in the section on "Ruth and the Books of Samuel" in the previous chapter).

Solomon's large harem included women from Moab, and he built a temple to the Moabite god Chemosh for them near Jerusalem (1 Kgs 11:1-8). This shrine to Chemosh survived for around three hundred years until Josiah destroyed it (2 Kgs 23:13). Thus according to Israelite tradition the country of Moab had a detrimental effect on Israelite life in terms of both territory and religious influence.

The story of Israel's relations with Moab is also available to us from a Moabite perspective through the testimony of the Moabite Stone. Discovered in 1868, the stone confirms that Chemosh was the national god of Moab and that there was conflict with Israel. Earlier defeats by Israel are regarded by Mesha, the king who commissioned the stone, as evidence that Chemosh was angry with his people. The stone celebrates Moab's independence from Israel. The story of Ruth becomes all the more surprising when we read it in the context of the hostility between the two countries — a hostility witnessed to not only by the biblical text but also by the archaeological discovery of the Moabite Stone.

Redemption

The story of Ruth is about a Moabite widow surrounded by Israelites and far from home. She was rescued by the generosity and love of a powerful man in that society who gained acceptance for her and pleaded her case in a legal setting at the city gate. Although we might use terminology such as "rescued" or "protected" to describe Boaz's actions, the book of Ruth uses the term "redeemed."

The Hebrew root for the concept of redemption is גאל/*g'l*. It occurs twenty-one times in the short book of Ruth and is even found five times in one verse (4:6). The first occurrence is at a turning point of the book, where Ruth returned from her first day of gleaning and told Naomi that she had been in the field of Boaz. Naomi, for the first time, responded positively with a sense of gratitude, explaining to Ruth that this man Boaz was a close relative of the family, "one of our redeemers" (2:20). This information is disclosed to the reader to build up our expectations that this is the way that Naomi and Ruth will be provided for. However, at this stage Boaz is presented only as "one of our redeemers," literally "from among our redeemers."

The root *g'l*, "redeem," occurs seven times in the conversation between Ruth and Boaz at the threshing floor, and there can be no doubt that redemption is the main theme related to this encounter. Ruth uses the term only once as she reminds Boaz of his responsibility. However, Boaz uses the root six times as he explains to Ruth that indeed he is a redeemer, but there is a closer redeemer who must be given first option; if he refuses, then Boaz promises on oath that he will act as redeemer (3:9-13).

However, the most concentrated use of the root *g'l* is found in the conversation between Boaz and the unknown redeemer. The root is used twelve times in eight verses, providing a clear focus and an unmistakable emphasis on the theme of redemption. The final occurrence is in the context of the women of Bethlehem praising YHWH that he has not left Naomi without a "redeemer" (4:14).

What, then, or who has been redeemed, and what precisely did it mean to be redeemed? It is clear that Boaz speaks about redeeming Ruth (3:13). However, in his conversation with the other redeemer, Boaz invites him to redeem the land (4:4), and finally the women of Bethlehem declare that God has not left Naomi without a redeemer (4:14). Thus there are references to the redemption of Ruth, the land, and Naomi. Regulations about the redemption of land are mentioned above in the section on "The Theme of Land" but are repeated here in the wider context of redemption.

> And in all the country you possess, you shall allow a redemption of the land.
>
> If your brother becomes poor and sells part of his property, then his nearest redeemer shall come and redeem what his brother has sold. If a man has no one to redeem it and then himself becomes prosperous and finds sufficient means to redeem it, let him calculate the years since he sold it and pay back the balance to the man to whom he sold it, and then return to his property. (Lev 25:24-27 ESV)

These land-redemption laws outlined in Leviticus protected a family's land from the grasp of wealthy landowners by preventing them from buying large swathes of land during hard times when land was cheap. According to

Leviticus, if a family had to sell their land to avoid poverty, then it was possible for that land to be bought back again either by the original owner or by a close relative. The act of buying back the land was called "redemption," and the person who carried out this act was called the "redeemer." The outworking of the law can be seen in the book of Jeremiah, where the act of buying back the land on the brink of war was seen as an act of faith and a symbol of hope (Jer 32:7). In cases where land was not redeemed, it was safeguarded by the prohibition of permanent land sales. The maximum lease was forty-nine years, since every fiftieth year the land should return to its original owner.[28]

Although the legal references to redemption relate to land, the concept had a wider application, and there are many references to the redemption of people. For example, in Genesis the patriarch Jacob speaks about his life as redemption. When he was blessing Joseph's sons, he referred to the "angel who has redeemed me from all evil" (Gen 48:16 ESV).[29] As Gerhard von Rad points out, the use of this term "redeem," which derives from the realm of family law, identifies YHWH as "the closest relative, prepared to redeem man."[30]

In Exodus two references describe the deliverance from Egypt as redemption (Exod 6:6; 15:13). YHWH acts as the near kinsman of Israel who delivers them from their enemies. The book of Ruth sheds light on this use of the concept of redemption and shows the significance of the relationship between the redeemer and the redeemed. By characterizing the deliverance from Egypt as redemption, the text is declaring that YHWH was in a close relationship with his people, and the act of deliverance was both the result of that relationship and the establishment of an even closer relationship. A parallel with Ruth can be seen clearly: following redemption her relationship with Boaz became closer through marriage, while following the deliverance from Egypt Israel's relationship with YHWH was confirmed and deepened through the covenant at Sinai.

Moreover, the theme of redemption is developed in detail in the latter part of the book of Isaiah, where in the context of the nation being restored after the exile, YHWH frequently refers to himself as the redeemer of Jacob/Israel (e.g., Isa 43:1; 44:6, 22-24). Again the idea of a relationship between the redeemer and the redeemed is in focus. In these passages God's role of redeemer includes not only the rescue of his people from their enemies but also the forgiveness of their sins.

---

28. See McKeown, "Land, Fertility, Famine."

29. The NIV translates this phrase as "the Angel who has delivered me from all harm." However, this obscures the use of the technical term "redeem," which most modern translations use.

30. Gerhard von Rad, *Genesis*, 413.

I have blotted out your transgressions like a cloud and your sins like mist; return to me, for I have redeemed you. Sing, O heavens, for the LORD has done it; shout, O depths of the earth; break forth into singing, O mountains, O forest, and every tree in it! For the LORD has redeemed Jacob, and will be glorified in Israel. (Isa 44:22-23 ESV)

The concept also applied at a personal level in Job and Psalms. The reference in Job is the well-known affirmation, "I know that my redeemer lives" (Job 19:25). The psalmist also expresses personal faith in God as redeemer. These references to God as redeemer clearly apply the concept in a wider sense than simply the redemption of land. It is the psalmist's life or soul that needs to be redeemed (Ps 69:18; cf. 72:14). Thus it need not surprise us that in the book of Ruth the land needs to be redeemed and also the people involved need redemption — Ruth and Naomi. Redemption in their case involved not rescuing them from an enemy but also saving them from poverty. There is no legislation in Leviticus that exactly matches what Boaz did, but the book of Ruth was not written as a legal document and probably reflects a wider custom.

The theme of redemption is prominent in the NT,[31] which describes the work of Christ using redemption terminology and symbolism. Scholars use the concept of redemption in two main ways. First, it is used as a general term for salvation through Jesus Christ. This approach is exemplified in the work of John Murray, who commences his book on redemption with, "The accomplishment of redemption is concerned with what has been generally called the atonement."[32]

However, a second approach to redemption is more nuanced and uses the term to denote only one aspect of salvation, and this is how the concept is used in the NT. As Gary Shogren explains, "While moderns may speak of redemption as a metaphor for the entire saving act, the NT writers used it precisely in the context of well-known social customs."[33] According to Shogren, "the social background of slave redemption provides a useful key to understanding the NT imagery."[34] Robert Hubbard also draws attention to slave

---

31. I am grateful to Dr. Graham Cheesman for his guidance and help with this section.

32. John Murray, *Redemption Accomplished and Applied*, 9. However, Murray also explains how the concept of redemption is used in a more specific sense: "The idea of redemption must not be reduced to the general notion of deliverance. The language of redemption is the language of purchase and more specifically of ransom. And ransom is the securing of a release by the payment of a price," 42.

33. Gary S. Shogren, "Redemption (NT)," 655.

34. Ibid.

redemption as underlying the understanding of redemption in the NT, but he emphasizes the influence of the OT on the imagery and in particular "the exodus from Egypt."[35]

Paul quotes Isaiah's prophecy (59:20) that "a Redeemer will come to Zion" (ESV), with slight but significant changes, and argues that Jesus is the fulfillment of this prophecy (Rom 11:26). Paul develops the theme of redemption by emphasizing that Christ's role is to liberate those who are enslaved to sin and under the curse imposed by the law (Gal 3:13; 4:3-5; cf. Rom 3:24-25). As Howard Marshall observes, "the accent lies on the deliverance of sinners and their entry into freedom, and the metaphor used is that of the ransoming of slaves."[36] Paul's use of this metaphor emphasizes the immense cost of redemption and shows that the liberated slaves now belong to the one who paid such a high price to set them free (1 Cor 6:20; 7:23). The cost of redemption is elucidated in 1 Peter, where the price that is paid is "the precious blood of Christ" (1 Pet 1:19; see also Col 1:14; Titus 2:14; Rev 5:9; 14:3-4). According to Hubbard, "Jesus' death produces a new spiritual paradox: slaves 'bought with a price' are not free but are slaves to a new owner."[37] As Marshall puts it, "paradoxically they are God's slaves and yet at the same time his freedmen (1 Cor 7:22)."[38]

Thus the NT draws mainly on the exodus theme of redemption as liberation of captives, and there is no specific reference to Boaz and Ruth. The importance of the book of Ruth is that it gives the clearest anecdotal evidence of how the concept of redemption could affect everyday life in Israel. It shows a kinsman redeemer in action and the effectiveness of such a role in providing for those in need.

Redemption has always been a significant concept in Jewish thought and has influenced Jewish theology and life. As Zvi Yaron explains, "There are prayers for redemption and there are benedictions in which God is praised as the redeemer of Israel. There are anxious prayers for deliverance from affliction and stress, and there are expressions of confident hope and even assurance that the redemption will be fulfilled."[39] In Jewish thought it is the exodus from Egypt that is the source and motivation of the theology of redemption. In particular the Passover service emphasizes that each participant should think of her- or himself as having personally been redeemed. "Not only our ancestors alone did the Holy One redeem but *us* as well, along with them, as it is written: 'And He

---

35. Hubbard, "Redemption," 718.
36. Howard Marshall, "Development of Concept of Redemption," 157.
37. Hubbard, "Redemption," 719.
38. Marshall, "Development," 157.
39. Zvi Yaron, "Redemption: A Contemporary Jewish Understanding," 169-79.

freed *us* from Egypt so as to take us and give us the land which He had sworn to our fathers.' "[40] Therefore, redemption, which is a very significant theological concept in the NT and also an enduring theme in Jewish thinking, is illustrated by the story of the redemption of Naomi, Ruth, and the land.

Universalism

Scholars have often noted that many passages in the OT have a universal theological dimension, whereas other passages have a much more nationalistic view focused on the people and land of Israel. Two men who are frequently labeled as nationalistic are Ezra and Nehemiah. In contrast, the books of Ruth and Jonah are labeled universalistic. This reflects the attitude of Ezra and Nehemiah to mixed marriages and particularly their insistence that Israelites should divorce foreign women. In sharp contrast, the book of Ruth is about a foreign woman who finds a warm welcome in Judah and who marries a well-respected citizen of Bethlehem. Moreover, Ruth's child becomes the grandfather of Israel's best-known king. This different emphasis is noted by Regina Schwartz:

> The Book of Ruth seems to offer an alternative to the vision of constraints in Ezra. Ezra's fear of losing property was coupled to his demand to reject foreign wives, and that sense of scarcity, of land, of wives, was in turn joined to a particularist monotheism. In contrast, Boaz feeds the stranger and gains a foreign wife, thereby endorsing a vision of plenitude and of fullness in monotheism.[41]

Ezra and Nehemiah show an attitude to foreigners that appears to be entirely different from the whole atmosphere of the book of Ruth. Although Ruth is a foreigner from Moab, she is welcomed by Boaz and eventually highly acclaimed by the people of Bethlehem. The story of Ruth moves toward the marriage of Ruth to Boaz, but in the books of Ezra and Nehemiah there is a strong emphasis on divorcing the foreigners.

The perceived different treatment of foreigners in Ezra and Nehemiah compared to the treatment of Ruth has led some scholars to conclude that the book of Ruth was written as a robust and critical response to the nationalism of Ezra and Nehemiah. One of the main passages is as follows:

40. *Passover Haggadah,* ed. Herbert Bronstein, 57.
41. Regina M. Schwartz, *Curse of Cain,* 90.

In those days also I saw the Jews who had married women of Ashdod, Ammon, and Moab. And half of their children spoke the language of Ashdod, and they could not speak the language of Judah, but the language of each people. And I confronted them and cursed them and beat some of them and pulled out their hair. And I made them take oath in the name of God, saying, "You shall not give your daughters to their sons, or take their daughters for your sons or for yourselves. Did not Solomon king of Israel sin on account of such women? Among the many nations there was no king like him, and he was beloved by his God, and God made him king over all Israel. Nevertheless, foreign women made even him to sin. Shall we then listen to you and do all this great evil and act treacherously against our God by marrying foreign women?" (Neh 13:23-27 ESV)

In the light of the exclusive attitude of Nehemiah, Michael Goulder describes the book of Ruth as "a highly skilled counterblast" to the teaching of Ezra/Nehemiah.[42] This view is echoed by Irmtraud Fischer: "I agree with those exegetes who think that the book of Ruth is a tendentious, if not a polemic, piece of work against the attempts of the books of Ezra and Nehemiah to reject mixed marriages."[43] Horst Dietrich Preuss expresses a widely held view:

The books of Ruth and Jonah oppose the narrowness of the postexilic community. On the one hand, even an ancestress of David is derived from Moab (Ruth 4:7) and also is spoken about in a positive way. On the other hand, heathen sailors offer better prayers than does the Israelite prophet, while the evil city of Nineveh responds openly to his preaching.[44]

This view is based on the judgment that Ezra and Nehemiah treated the wives unfairly, which contrasts sharply with the way that Ruth was treated. However, we cannot ignore the different context of Ezra/Nehemiah when compared to Ruth. The undeniably harsh measures in Ezra/Nehemiah were designed to prevent the small community in Yehud (Judah) from losing its identity through syncretistic worship. The women who were targeted were not converts to faith in YHWH. This is not the situation in the book of Ruth. She became a proselyte, genuinely and without pressure. The situation encountered by Ezra/Nehemiah was that the Jewish men were following the gods of their wives, adopting their culture and speaking their language. None of these threats exists in the story

42. Michael D. Goulder, "Ruth: Homily on Deuteronomy 22–25?" 316.
43. Irmtraud Fischer, "Book of Ruth: 'Feminist' Commentary?" 34.
44. Horst Dietrich Preuss, *Old Testament Theology*, 2:293.

of Ruth, and the Israelite identity of Ruth's baby is fully protected since Naomi officially adopted the child. Although his mother was a Moabite, he was raised in a traditional Israelite home.

Murray Gow argues that Ruth's conversion to YHWH "tends to undermine the theory that the book was written to counter Ezra's and Nehemiah's rigid policy on mixed marriages."[45] His point is that there is nothing in the book of Ruth that Ezra or Nehemiah would have disagreed with, and he suggests that the book could even have been written by someone who supported their reforms. According to Gow, the book of Ruth justifies the marriage of Boaz to Ruth by showing that she had become part of the community at Bethlehem and a true believer in YHWH.[46]

Nevertheless, we must not underestimate the emphasis on Ruth's foreignness. Her Moabite origins are continually rehearsed throughout the book, ensuring that the reader is not allowed to forget that this is not an ordinary love story but a story that crosses international boundaries and that shows that parochial prejudice is no match for selfless humanity. Schwartz suggests that Ruth is not really a foreigner, and Boaz's generosity is for the sake of his own kin since his relative Naomi is the mother-in-law of Ruth. She comments,

> Yet even this vision of universal plenitude is compromised, ironically enough, by kinship, for the narrative takes pains to establish that in the end Ruth the Moabitess is not really a stranger after all, but a relative, so that Boaz's generous marriage that seemed to take in the poor foreigner is not fully to a foreigner. Boaz is a kinsman of Naomi, Ruth's mother-in-law.[47]

Although Schwartz is correct that the legal framework within which Boaz acts as redeemer relates to his family connections, his relationship with Ruth shows an attitude of acceptance to the foreigner Ruth before he knows very much about her, and his generosity was offered freely and without qualification. Boaz shows no inhibition or hesitation when he is told that the stranger in his field is from the land of Moab. Furthermore, the frequent references to Ruth as the Moabite in the text continually draw attention to her foreign origins in Moab. Even though Ruth was previously married to a relative of Boaz, this previous marriage took place in the land of Moab, and her marriage in Bethlehem reflected an attitude of openness and acceptance of someone from outside the close-knit community. This does reflect an outlook that is certainly more tol-

---

45. Gow, *Book of Ruth*, 131-32.
46. Ibid., 133.
47. Schwartz, *Curse of Cain*, 90.

erant than that of Ezra/Nehemiah. Yet the openness to a foreigner in the book of Ruth is very much in harmony with other passages of Scripture, especially Isaiah 40–66, which emphasizes Israel's mission to the nations that culminates when "all flesh shall come to worship" YHWH (66:23 ESV).

Schwartz warns about the possible abuse that can take place when the Bible is used to support one modern political view against another. This involves selecting various texts and wresting them from their context to marshal evidence that one particular political stance is more biblical than the other:

> Interpretations of biblical narratives have also been put to any and every political purpose. When universalism was needed, Deutero-Isaiah's sentiment that Israel is a light to the nations was useful. When particularism was in order, Ezra's inveighing against the foreigner would do. Since it seems to contain all things, it has been useful for all ends.[48]

Abusive interpretations of the text have undoubtedly taken place, particularly when one specific text has been promoted to support a cause without reference to its context and without cognizance of other passages that offer a different perspective and provide an overall balanced approach. We must always clearly distinguish between what the Bible teaches and how it has been interpreted. Many have sadly used the Bible to support racism, but as Schwartz points out, "the Bible itself is not 'racist,' although many people who read/interpret it have put it to such service."[49]

Therefore one is required to have a balanced approach to biblical texts that reflect the different circumstances in which they were written. The OT was not written as a political manual, but it was not produced in a vacuum. Rather it was written in the context of the cut and thrust of everyday life, and its writings reflect the prevailing socioeconomic and political context in which it was first composed. God's messages were revealed to people in a way that was relevant to the circumstances they faced. We can misinterpret that message if we divorce it from its context. The Bible represents the interaction with various circumstances, including national emergencies, and this is reflected in its diversity. It is true that some texts, such as Ruth and Jonah, represent an openness to foreign nations that is absent from other texts, such as Ezra/Nehemiah. However, these differences do not represent opposing worldviews or conflicting standpoints. Instead, they represent different aspects of OT theology appropriately contextualized. J. G. McConville correctly observes that in the OT the "political picture

---

48. Ibid., 8.
49. Ibid., 103.

changes with the exigencies that faced Israel at various times."[50] The books of Ruth and Jonah should not, therefore, be seen as a different approach from Ezra/Nehemiah. The message of the OT should be understood in the light of both approaches. The OT does not present an idealized picture of Israel; but, as McConville demonstrates, it portrays the nation reacting to events that required pragmatic approaches appropriate to each context.[51]

In the context of the book of Ruth, we can conclude that its emphasis on the acceptance of a foreigner is not out of harmony with other OT texts, and it provides a useful reminder that the Bible evokes a universal vision of all humanity worshiping YHWH.

Feminist Studies

Ruth — A Woman's Book

Phyllis Trible begins her essay on the book of Ruth with the oft-quoted words, "A man's world tells a woman's story."[52] This sentence reflects both what attracts feminist authors to the book of Ruth and also what repels them. Many feminist studies find a great deal to applaud in the book of Ruth. For example, it describes resourceful women who take the initiative to provide for themselves. However, there are also many negative aspects in the book from a feminist perspective. Ruth and Naomi live in a man's world in which survival depends on finding a husband. Women may take the initiative, but it is men who make the final decisions. To add insult to injury, from a feminist perspective, the concluding genealogy is entirely male. Ruth is indeed a woman's story, but the world that the story depicts is one in which women were not always treated well. This helps to explain the ambivalence of some feminist writers to the book. Although its heroine is a woman, the predicament in which she finds herself reflects the prevailing patriarchal society. Trible shows clearly how this male dominance is evident in the book of Ruth. She points out that in the first verse of the book, the children of Naomi and Elimelech are described as "*his* children," not "*their* children" (Ruth 1:1).[53] She also observes that Naomi's predicament was a product of the society in which she lived. Referring to Naomi's bereavement of the three men in her life, Trible comments,

50. J. G. McConville, *God and Earthly Power*, 30.

51. In relation to the diversity of the OT, McConville comments, "The Old Testament does not present any of the forms taken by Israel as ideal, for each is portrayed in its vulnerability, not only to external forces but also to inner corruption" (ibid., 30).

52. Trible, *God and Rhetoric*, 166.

53. Ibid., 167.

Naomi stands alone. The narration focuses entirely upon her, but it avoids her name. "The woman," it says, "was bereft of her two children and her husband" (v. 5). From wife to widow, from mother to no-mother, this female is stripped of all identity. The security of husband and children, which a male-dominated culture affords its women, is hers no longer.[54]

Nevertheless, in spite of their low status, Trible, referring to Ruth 2, observes that "in their own right the women shape their story. They plan (v. 2); they execute (vv. 3-17); and they evaluate (vv. 18-22)."[55] So while the book of Ruth is attractive to feminist writers because of its depiction of women who take the initiative, its patriarchal setting makes it less attractive.

Thus, as Joseph W. Blotz comments: "The Book of Ruth has been an object of contention for many feminist scholars of the Bible. While recognizing the great strides the book makes on behalf of women, scholars also recognize how far the work on a whole has fallen short of some feminist ideals."[56] Madipoane J. Masenya expresses a similar view: "Feminists are divided regarding the book of Ruth. Some are enthusiastic about the book, taking Ruth to be a strong, independent character. Her relationship to Naomi is seen as an example of a voluntary bonding between females. Others, however, see Ruth and the book as submitting to the agenda of males."[57]

One of the strengths of feminist writers' work is the sensitive way that they help us to understand the strengths and weaknesses of the characters. Trible, for example, shows that although Naomi gives advice and does so strongly, the younger women are in charge of their own destinies. Although Orpah took her mother-in-law's advice, it was her decision to do so. Orpah made up her mind and acted accordingly, showing decisiveness and displaying evidence of the ability to think independently. Trible concludes, "Orpah does the expected, Ruth the unexpected. As a result, both emerge as persons. Use of their names, for the first time since the introduction (v. 4), clinches this point."[58]

Several scholars, including Adrien Bledstein, draw attention to the suggestion of S. D. Goitein that not only is Ruth a woman's story but also it may have been written by "a wise, old woman."[59] Bledstein attempts to show that

---

54. Ibid.

55. Ibid., 180.

56. Joseph W. Blotz, "Bitterness and Friendship," 47.

57. Madipoane J. Masenya, "Ngwetši (Bride)," 82.

58. Trible, *God and Rhetoric*, 172, commenting on Ruth 1:4.

59. Adrien J. Bledstein, "Female Companionships," 117. Bledstein is quoting from S. D. Goitein, "Women as Creators of Biblical Genres." See also Fokkelein van Dijk-Hemmes, *Ruth and Women's Culture*, 137.

if we assume that the book is written by a woman, our approach to it and the lessons we learn will be enhanced: "Reading Ruth through the filter of imagining the book as written by a wise woman with a sense of humor and irony changes what we see."[60]

A number of scholars draw attention to the unexpected advice of Naomi to Orpah and Ruth that each should return to her *mother's* house. In a similar context, Judah instructs Tamar to return to her *father's* house (Gen 38:11). As Ilona Rashkow points out, "Naomi's intended destination for her daughters-in-law, 'each to her mother's house,' is striking given the overriding importance of 'father's house' throughout the male-oriented Hebrew Bible."[61] Carol Meyers presents an important and fascinating study of this phrase (mother's house). Rather than look at how the term is used in the book of Ruth in isolation, she studies it in the context of its use elsewhere in the Hebrew Bible. Meyers concludes that this phrase supports the possibility that the book of Ruth may have been written by a woman.

> The fact that the phrase "mother's house" appears here in a brilliant, resoundingly female tale should help us to refocus the investigation of what it signifies so that it may stand on its own as a legitimate social term and as a signifier of a woman's text.
>
> . . . The major goal of my examination of this phrase will be to show how, because of certain similarities of literary genre and social context between Ruth and the few other passages where the term occurs, this verse and perhaps all of Ruth can be heard as Israelite women's language.[62]

Meyers studies the other passages in the Hebrew Bible that refer to "mother's house." In Gen 24:8 Abraham's servant had asked Rebekah whether there was room in her father's house, and she confirms that there is; but then she runs to tell her "mother's house" about the stranger. Of course, if her father was dead then this could explain the difference, but the text as it stands suggests otherwise (24:50). It seems likely that when the servant speaks, he does so from a man's point of view, but the text itself is written from a woman's standpoint. Meyers sets this in the context of the prominence of Rebekah in the narrative: she plays a very active role, overshadowing not only the other women but also her husband, Isaac.

Concerning the two occurrences in the Song of Songs (3:4; 8:2), Meyers

---

60. Bledstein, "Female Companionships," 117.
61. Ilona Rashkow, "Ruth: Discourse of Power," 29.
62. Carol Meyers, "Returning Home," 92.

observes: "Not only is a woman's voice heard more directly in the Song of Songs than anywhere else in the Hebrew Bible, but also its major character is a woman, as are many of the supporting cast of characters. References to other females far outnumber mentions of men."[63] Thus Meyers concludes that the passages where "mother's house" occurs "share certain fundamental characteristics, among which are:

1. *A woman's story is being told. . . .*
2. *A wisdom association is present. . . .*
3. *Women are agents in their own destiny. . . .*
4. *The agency of women affects others. . . .*
5. *The setting is domestic. . . .*
6. *Marriage is involved.*

Meyers emphasizes that all these features "involve a female perspective on issues which elsewhere in the Hebrew Bible are viewed from the male perspective that dominates Scripture."[64] She sees this as an accurate reflection of the role that women played in ancient societies. Particularly in matters relating to marriage, the role of women was important and active and may be somewhat obscured by the prominence of men in the authoring of the texts. Thus her argument is not that a woman definitely wrote the book of Ruth but that a woman's perspective is clearly seen not only in Ruth but also in the other passages where "mother's house" is mentioned.

Richard Bauckham contends that while it is impossible to know whether the author of Ruth was male or female, the book is written from "an ancient Israelite woman's perspective on ancient Israelite society."[65] He thinks that this female perspective is maintained until the last few verses of the book, when "the male voice speaks" in the patrilineal genealogy. According to Bauckham the book originally ended with v. 17.

Less reticence about female authorship is shown by Bledstein: "I suggest we think of this narrator as Tamar, the daughter of David, who could have written during the latter part of David's and the early years of Solomon's reigns. She was the great-great-granddaughter of Ruth, Naomi and Boaz, and descended from the earlier Tamar of Genesis."[66] Tamar's life was an unenviable example of how things could go badly wrong for a woman, even if she was a daughter

---

63. Ibid., 103.
64. Ibid., 109-10.
65. Richard Bauckham, "Book of Ruth," 30-31.
66. Bledstein, "Female Companionships," 132.

of King David. She experienced rape, abuse, and neglect. In spite of his standing as national protector and hero, her father had done nothing to protect her and did not even punish the one who caused her so much grief. If Bledstein is correct that in her later years she became an author, it would be a pleasing conclusion to a turbulent life. However, lack of evidence either way leaves this as an interesting hypothesis that brings us no closer to any certainty about the authorship of the book of Ruth.

At the endgame in chapter 4, as the men hold their meeting at the gateway to Bethlehem, Trible draws attention to how the story is dominated by the males — they hold the discussions and they make the decisions. She highlights how Boaz's presentation of the facts is based on male interests only. Of course, Naomi and Ruth are interested parties, but the focus of the proceedings is on "the restoration of the name of the dead to his inheritance."[67] She poignantly concludes that "the men shifted emphasis from justice for living females to justice for dead males."[68] Naomi's view is different and has to do with practical concerns such as finding "rest" for her daughter-in-law. Thus the male-dominated society fulfills the needs of the women but only as a means to fulfill the men's goals.

The interaction between the main female characters is carefully delineated by studying their conversations. As Meyers observes, "No other book in the Hebrew Bible has a higher ratio of dialogue to narrative text."[69] Rashkow also highlights the importance of discourse in the book of Ruth: "56 of the 85 verses report speech acts." Furthermore, it is the discourse of the female characters that "carries the narrative forward."[70] The book could have been written without dialogue, and the actions of the main characters could have been described without putting it in their own words. However, without the dialogue we would not have the same insight into the characters' motives, emotions, and feelings.[71]

Rashkow describes Naomi as the "central character in terms of discourse."[72] In her speech to Orpah and Ruth, Naomi's own bitterness and sense of despair are revealed, and as Rashkow points out, she is "more biting in her sarcasm than she need be if her only desire is to express concern for her two daughters-in-law."[73] However, perhaps it is Ruth's character that is elucidated most by a study of her speech. "In her relationship with Naomi Ruth is deter-

---

67. Trible, *God and Rhetoric,* 192.

68. Ibid., 194.

69. Meyers, "Returning Home," 92-93.

70. Rashkow, "Ruth: Discourse of Power," 26.

71. This view is argued clearly by Carol Meyers, "Returning Home," 93.

72. Rashkow, "Ruth: Discourse of Power," 28.

73. Ibid., 30.

mined and assertive, but of relatively few words; with Boaz, Ruth maintains a higher level of formality but is quite articulate, almost too talkative."[74] However, it is not just what the characters say that is important but also their silences. The most prominent silence in the book occurs when the two women arrive in Bethlehem. Why does Naomi not mention Ruth? Rashkow suggests that "Naomi's silence, as powerful as her words, seems to emphasize an alienation between the two women."[75]

Many consider the relationship between the two women to be particularly ambiguous. This ambiguity is clearly highlighted by Cheryl Exum, who draws attention to the intimacy between the two women and to the verbal correspondence between Ruth 1:14 and Gen 2:24. The same root דבק/*dbq*, "to cling," is used in relation to a man leaving his father and mother to be with his wife. The word is translated in various ways in Gen 2:24: "hold fast" (ESV), "be united to" (NIV), "clings to" (NRSV). The use of the same word in connection with the relationship between Ruth and Naomi leads Exum to describe the relationship as "her symbolic marriage to Naomi."[76] Jon Berquist also highlights the link with Gen 2:24 and points out that the term דבק/*dbq* "refers to the male role in initiating marriage." He comments, "Outside of Ruth, the term 'cling' never describes a woman's act. This makes Ruth 1.14 all the more striking. When Ruth clings to Naomi, Ruth takes the male role in initiating a relationship of formal commitment, similar to marriage."[77] However, we must be careful not to read too much into this reference to Ruth clinging to Naomi. It should be understood in the context of the entire book since *dbq*, "to cling," is used on three other occasions (2:8, 21, 23). These references are to the advice of Boaz, echoed by Naomi, that Ruth should "cling" or "stay close" to the women workers and to Ruth's underlying desire to "cling" to the young men! These occurrences of the verb *dbq* seem to highlight Ruth's precarious situation; she does need someone to "cling" to, but she must make her choice carefully.

Only two books are named after women in the Hebrew Bible: Ruth and Esther. Ruth is unique in that it is the name of a foreign woman from a country that had a history of conflict with Israel. Indeed, the book of Ruth is the only book in the Hebrew Bible that is named after a non-Israelite. As Fischer observes, "The book of Ruth was never called 'the book of Boaz' or 'the book of Elimelech.' Its title has always had a preference for female experience. Hardly any other book of the Bible manages to express the 'female voice' as authenti-

---

74. Ibid., 29.
75. Ibid., 33.
76. Cheryl Exum, *Plotted, Shot, and Painted*, 145.
77. Jon L. Berquist, "Role Dedifferentiation," 26-27.

cally as Ruth does."[78] The book of Ruth is important for feminist studies because it gives women an opportunity to express themselves. The book seems to be written from a woman's point of view. There are men involved, but the main focus of the book is on women, their needs, problems, and aspirations.

Missiological Significance

Israel's mission to the surrounding nations is a theme that is easily overlooked. Yet its significance in the OT is inescapable. According to A. J. Köstenberger, "mission is an exceedingly important motif pervading virtually the entire course of biblical revelation."[79] The programmatic call of Abraham was focused ultimately on the blessing of the nations (Gen 12:1-3), and the purpose of the exodus event was to establish Israel as God's "treasured possession among all peoples," and they were to become "a kingdom of priests and a holy nation" (Exod 19:5-6). Israel's mission was emphasized particularly with reference to the postexilic community in which God's house became "a house of prayer for all peoples" (Isa 56:7).

The emphasis on mission, with the exception of Jonah, should not be confused with the modern concept of cross-cultural mission. Rather, as Köstenberger argues, "as the recipient of the divine blessings, the nation is to exalt God in its life and worship, attracting individuals from among the nations historically by incorporation and eschatologically by ingathering."[80] In the time of the judges — the period to which the book of Ruth relates — the people of Israel had clearly failed in this mission since "everyone did what was right in his own eyes" (Judg 17:6; 21:25). In this context there is evidence that the concept of Israel's role as a witness to YHWH was an important issue in the book of Ruth, providing a contrast with the general picture given in the book of Judges. Early in the story of Ruth there is clear emphasis on the impact of Israel's existence on other nations, since news reached Moab that YHWH had provided food for his people. That this is not just an incidental reference is underlined by the repetition of "Moab" in 1:6: "Then she arose with her daughters-in-law to return from the country of Moab, for she had heard in the fields of Moab that the LORD had visited his people and given them food" (ESV). Thus the events occurring in Israel were newsworthy in the land of Moab and the credit was given to YHWH.

Although the date when the book of Ruth was written is uncertain,

78. Fischer, "Book of Ruth: 'Feminist' Commentary?" 24.
79. A. J. Köstenberger, "Mission," 663.
80. Ibid., 664.

Nancy J. Thomas suggests that the missiological emphasis of the book would have been an important message for the postexilic era:

> I propose that the book of Ruth did, indeed, communicate appropriately in the context of post-exilic Israel. The needs of the people for spiritual restoration, as well as for physical and national survival, fueled the writer's intention to encourage their faith in a God who restores. Intention and theme were those demanded by the context. The author was affirming old values and promises, reminding Israel of her calling and identity, with a view to realizing these in a completely new and challenging situation.[81]

Furthermore, Ruth's foreignness is obviously a leitmotif in the book, and the same story told about an Israelite woman would not have had the same impact. Seven times we are reminded about Ruth's foreign origin: 1:4, 22; 2:2, 6, 10; 4:5, 10. In the book of Judges, Moabites and Israelites killed each other, but in the book of Ruth the Moabites provided food and shelter for an Israelite family, and the Israelites provided a secure home for a Moabite woman who embraced not only her Israelite mother-in-law but also her God. As Thomas comments, "The depiction of Ruth the Moabitess as a convert to the faith, a woman of worth, and the grandmother of David certainly conveyed the message of God's love for all people. This is a missiologically relevant message."[82] Thus the book of Ruth makes a contribution to missiological studies by the contrasting attitude that it shows to the people of the land of Moab and in particular to a person from that country who was willing to embrace the religion, people, and culture of Israel.

Elsewhere I have argued that the failure of many of the characters to participate in God's mission is an important theme in the book of Genesis.[83] This failure was particularly evident in the stories of Jacob, in which there is no evidence that Jacob and his sons considered being a blessing to the nations as a priority. In Jacob's dealing with Laban, Esau, the Shechemites, or the Hittites, he showed much more evidence of selfish concerns than of a sense of mission. The story of Joseph involves a foreign nation, but the emphasis is on survival rather than on mission. While Joseph provided famine relief for Egypt and the surrounding nations, this is not presented as mission since the people were charged for the food and those with no money were enslaved (Gen 47:13-21). In contrast, the characters in the book of Ruth are exemplary in their

---

81. Nancy J. Thomas, "Weaving the Words," 164.
82. Ibid.
83. McKeown, *Genesis,* 324.

approach to a foreign woman. Although they had their own self-interest and their own agendas, there was an openness and generosity that provides a breath of fresh air especially against the lawless and self-centered background painted in the book of Judges.

Conclusion

The book of Ruth is more than just a charming story. Set in the context of Genesis, Judges, and the books of Samuel, it provides an important perspective on family life in OT times. Although the book is not usually classified as wisdom literature, it certainly provides an example of the kind of pragmatic wisdom that we find in this type of literature. It shows how people coped with difficult situations and overcame seemingly insurmountable obstacles. The book also provides an important perspective on relationships with people from the surrounding nations. Ruth's story is a breath of fresh air and a pleasant reminder that Israel did not always regard foreigners as enemies in OT times.

The book's theological importance could easily be overlooked, but in spite of its format as a short story, it provides a framework for the discussion of significant theological issues such as universalism, the hiddenness of God, redemption, and land. The absence of special divine revelation or prophetic pronouncements in the book make it a good starting point for discussing how human beings can relate to God in normal circumstances.

However, the book of Ruth is important not only theologically but also historically. The book's historical perspective is significant in the way that it presents Israel's greatest king as the grandson of a poor Moabite woman. The nation that traced its origins to slavery in Egypt also included a foreign woman in its royal family tree. Furthermore, the attitude to women in the book of Ruth is in sharp contrast to the way in which kings like David and Solomon treated their women. Ruth is an important book showing that the behavior of Israel toward women as recorded in the books of Judges, Samuel, and Kings should not be recognized as the norm for followers of YHWH. The book of Ruth provides a commentary on the treatment of women in the OT.

As a book in our canon of Scripture, the book of Ruth provides allusions to several other books in the OT. Ruth helpfully sheds light on those texts and highlights the issues that they raised for the first readers. It is remarkable that such a short book successfully provides a cohesive link between Israel's earlier history and the period of the monarchy. Yet none of this can explain the continued popularity and appeal of the book today. Perhaps this lies in the fact that it is "an everyday story of country folk."

Bibliography

Alexander, T. D. *From Paradise to the Promised Land*. 2nd ed. Grand Rapids: Baker Academic, 2002.

———. "Seed." *NDBT* 769-72.

Alter, Robert. *The World of Biblical Literature*. London: SPCK, 1992.

Anderson, A. A. "The Marriage of Ruth." *JSS* 23.2 (1978): 171-83.

Balentine, Samuel E. *The Hidden God: The Hiding of the Face of God in the Old Testament*. Oxford: Oxford University Press, 1983.

Bar-Efrat, Shimon. *Narrative Art in the Bible*. JSOTSup 70. Sheffield: Almond, 1989.

Barth, Karl. *Church Dogmatics*. Vol. 3, part 3: *The Doctrine of Creation*. Trans. G. W. Bromiley and R. J. Ehrlich. Ed. G. W. Bromiley and T. F. Torrance. Edinburgh: T&T Clark, 1960.

Barton, John. *The Spirit and the Letter: Studies in the Biblical Canon*. London: SPCK, 1997.

Bauckham, Richard. "The Book of Ruth and the Possibility of a Feminist Canonical Hermeneutic." *BibInt* 5.1 (1997): 29-45.

Baylis, Charles P. "Naomi in the Book of Ruth in Light of the Mosaic Covenant." *BSac* 161.644 (2004): 413-31.

Beattie, D. R. G. "The Book of Ruth as Evidence for Israelite Legal Practice." *VT* 24.3 (1974): 251-67.

———. *Jewish Exegesis of the Book of Ruth*. JSOTSup 2. Sheffield: JSOT Press, 1977.

———. "Ruth, Book of." In *Dictionary of Biblical Interpretation*. Ed. John H. Hayes, 2:426-28. 2 vols. Nashville: Abingdon, 1999.

———. "Ruth III." *JSOT* 5 (1978): 39-48.

Berger, Yitzhak. "Ruth and the David-Bathsheba Story: Allusions and Contrasts." *JSOT* 33.4 (2009): 433-52.

———. "Ruth and Inner-Biblical Allusion: The Case of 1 Samuel 25." *JBL* 128.2 (2009): 253-72.

Berlin, Adele. *Poetics and Interpretation of Biblical Narrative*. Bible and Literature 9. Sheffield: Almond, 1983.

Bernstein, Moshe J. "Two Multivalent Readings in the Ruth Narrative." *JSOT* 50 (1991): 15-26.

Berquist, Jon L. "Role Dedifferentiation in the Book of Ruth." *JSOT* 57 (1993): 23-37.

Biran, Avraham. "Tel Dan." In *New Encyclopedia of Archaeological Excavations in the Holy Land*. Ed. Ephraim Stern, 1:323-32. Jerusalem: Carta, 1993.

Bledstein, Adrien J. "Female Companionships: If the Book Were Written by a Woman. . . ."

In *A Feminist Companion to Ruth.* Ed. Athalya Brenner, 116-33. FBC 1/3. Sheffield: Sheffield Academic Press, 1993.

Block, Daniel I. "Ruth." In *Judges, Ruth,* 587-737. New American Commentary. Nashville: Broadman & Holman, 1999.

Blotz, Joseph W. "Bitterness and Friendship: A Feminist Exegesis of the Book of Ruth." *Currents in Theology and Mission* 32 (2005): 47-54.

Bovell, Carlos. "Symmetry, Ruth and Canon." *JSOT* 28.2 (2003): 175-91.

Brenner, Athalya. "Naomi and Ruth." *VT* 33.4 (1983): 385-97.

———, ed. *Ruth and Esther.* FCB 2/3. Sheffield: Sheffield Academic Press, 1999.

———. "Ruth as a Foreign Worker and the Politics of Exogamy." In *Ruth and Esther.* Ed. Athalya Brenner, 158-62. FCB 2/3. Sheffield: Sheffield Academic Press, 1999.

Britt, Brian. "Death, Social Conflict, and the Barley Harvest in the Hebrew Bible." *Journal of Hebrew Scriptures* 5 (2004): 1-28.

Bronner, Leila Leah. "A Thematic Approach to Ruth in Rabbinic Literature." In *A Feminist Companion to Ruth.* Ed. Athalya Brenner, 146-69. FCB 1/3. Sheffield: Sheffield Academic Press, 1993.

Bronstein, Herbert, ed. *A Passover Haggadah: The New Union Haggadah Prepared by the Central Conference of American Rabbis.* Rev. ed. New York: Viking, 1982.

Brueggemann, Walter. *The Land: Place as Gift, Promise, and Challenge in Biblical Faith.* 2nd ed. OBT. Minneapolis: Fortress, 2002.

Bush, Frederic W. "Ruth." In *Ruth, Esther,* 2-268. Word Biblical Commentary 9. Dallas: Word, 1996.

Campbell, Edward F., Jr. "Naomi, Boaz, and Ruth: *Hesed* (חסד) and Change." *Austin Seminary Bulletin* 105.2 (1990): 64-74.

———. *Ruth.* AB 7. Garden City, NY: Doubleday, 1975.

Coxon, Peter W. "Was Naomi a Scold?" *JSOT* 45 (1989): 25-37.

Darr, Katheryn Pfisterer. *Far More Precious than Jewels: Perspectives on Biblical Women.* Louisville: Westminster John Knox, 1991.

Davies, Eryl W. "Ruth IV 5 and the Duties of the *Gō'ēl.*" *VT* 33.2 (1983): 231-34.

De Waard, Jan, and Eugene A. Nida. *A Translator's Handbook on the Book of Ruth.* Helps for Translators 15. London: United Bible Societies, 1973.

Dempster, Stephen G. *Dominion and Dynasty: A Theology of the Hebrew Bible.* New Studies in Biblical Theology 15. Downers Grove, IL: InterVarsity Press, 2003.

Dijk-Hemmes, Fokkelein van. "Ruth: A Product of Women's Culture?" In *A Feminist Companion to Ruth.* Ed. Athalya Brenner, 134-39. FCB 1/3. Sheffield: Sheffield Academic Press, 1993.

Dillard, Raymond B., and Tremper Longman III. *An Introduction to the Old Testament.* Grand Rapids: Zondervan, 1995.

Eskenazi, Tamara Cohn, and Tikva Frymer-Kensky. *Ruth.* Jewish Publication Society Bible Commentary. Philadelphia: Jewish Publication Society, 2011.

Exum, J. Cheryl. *Plotted, Shot, and Painted: Cultural Representations of Biblical Women.* JSOTSup 215. Sheffield: Sheffield Academic Press, 1996.

Fewell, Danna Nolan, and David Miller Gunn. "Boaz, Pillar of Society: Measures of Worth in the Book of Ruth." *JSOT* 45 (1989): 45-59.

———. *Compromising Redemption: Relating Characters in the Book of Ruth.* Louisville: Westminster John Knox, 1990.

———. "Is Coxon a Scold? On Responding to the Book of Ruth." *JSOT* 45 (1989): 39-43.

———. "'A Son Is Born to Naomi!' Literary Allusions and Interpretation in the Book of Ruth." *JSOT* 40 (1988): 99-108.

Fisch, Harold. "Ruth and the Structure of Covenant History." *VT* 32.4 (1982): 425-37.

Fischer, Irmtraud. "The Book of Ruth as Exegetical Literature." *European Judaism* 40.2 (2007): 140-49.

———. "The Book of Ruth: A 'Feminist' Commentary to the Torah?" In *Ruth and Esther*. Ed. Athalya Brenner, 24-49. FCB 2/3. Sheffield: Sheffield Academic Press, 1999.

Fretheim, Terence E. *God and World in the Old Testament: A Relational Theology of Creation*. Nashville: Abingdon, 2005.

Glover, Neil. "Your People, My People: An Exploration of Ethnicity in Ruth." *JSOT* 33.3 (2009): 293-313.

Goitein, S. D. "Women as Creators of Biblical Genres." *Prooftexts* 8.1 (1988): 1-33.

Goldingay, John. *Men Behaving Badly*. Carlisle: Paternoster, 2000.

Goulder, Michael D. "Ruth: A Homily on Deuteronomy 22–25?" In *Of Prophets' Visions and the Wisdom of Sages: Essays in Honour of R. Norman Whybray on His Seventieth Birthday*. Ed. Heather A. McKay and David J. A. Clines, 307-19. JSOTSup 162. Sheffield: JSOT Press, 1993.

Gow, Murray D. *The Book of Ruth: Its Structure, Theme and Purpose*. London: Apollos, 1992.

———. "Ruth." In *Theological Interpretation of the Old Testament: A Book-by-Book Survey*. Ed. Kevin J. Vanhoozer, Craig G. Bartholomew, and Daniel J. Treier, 102-10. Grand Rapids: Baker Academic, 2008.

Grant, Reg. "Literary Structure in the Book of Ruth." *BSac* 148.592 (1991): 424-41.

Gray, John. *Joshua, Judges, Ruth*. New Century Bible Commentary. Repr., Grand Rapids: Eerdmans, 1986.

Green, Barbara. "The Plot of the Biblical Story of Ruth." *JSOT* 23 (1982): 55-68.

Grelot, Pierre. *What Are the Targums?* Collegeville, MN: Liturgical Press, 1992.

Grossman, Jonathan. "'Gleaning among the Ears' — 'Gathering among the Sheaves': Characterizing the Image of the Supervising Boy (Ruth 2)." *JBL* 126.4 (2007): 703-16.

Habel, Norman C. *The Land Is Mine: Six Biblical Land Ideologies*. OBT. Minneapolis: Fortress, 1995.

Hals, Ronald M. *The Theology of the Book of Ruth*. Facet Books. Philadelphia: Fortress, 1969.

Holmstedt, Robert D. *Ruth: A Handbook on the Hebrew Text*. Baylor Handbook on the Hebrew Bible. Waco: Baylor University Press, 2010.

Honig, Bonnie. "Ruth, the Model Emigrée: Mourning and the Symbolic Politics of Immigration." In *Ruth and Esther*. Ed. Athalya Brenner, 50-74. FCB 2/3. Sheffield: Sheffield Academic Press, 1999.

House, Paul R. *Old Testament Theology*. Downers Grove, IL: InterVarsity Press, 1998.

Hubbard, Robert L., Jr. *The Book of Ruth*. New International Commentary on the Old Testament. Grand Rapids: Eerdmans, 1988.

———. "Redemption." *NDBT* 716-20.

———. "Theological Reflections on Naomi's Shrewdness." *TynBul* 40.2 (1989): 283-92.

Hyman, Ronald T. "Questions and Changing Identity in the Book of Ruth." *Union Seminary Quarterly Review* 39.3 (1984): 189-201.

Köstenberger, A. J. "Mission." *NDBT* 663-68.

LaCocque, André. *Ruth*. Continental Commentary. Trans. K. C. Hanson. Minneapolis: Fortress, 2004.

Leggett, Donald A. *The Levirate and Goel Institutions in the Old Testament with Special Attention to the Book of Ruth*. Cherry Hill, NJ: Mack, 1974.

Levine, Étan. *The Aramaic Version of Ruth*. Analecta biblica 58. Rome: Biblical Institute Press, 1973.

Linafelt, Tod. "Ruth." In Tod Linafelt and Timothy K. Beal, *Ruth and Esther*, xi-90. Berit Olam. Collegeville, MN: Liturgical Press, 1999.

Lindström, Fredrik. *Suffering and Sin: Interpretations of Illness in the Individual Complaint Psalms*. Coniectanea biblica, Old Testament Series 37. Stockholm: Almquist & Wiksell, 1994.

McConville, J. G. *God and Earthly Power: An Old Testament Political Theology: Genesis–Kings*. London: T&T Clark, 2006.

McKeown, James. "Blessings and Curses." *DOTP* 83-87.

———. *Genesis*. Two Horizons Old Testament Commentary. Grand Rapids: Eerdmans, 2008.

———. "Land, Fertility, Famine." *DOTP* 487-91.

Magonet, Jonathan. "Rabbinic Readings of Ruth." *European Judaism* 40.2 (2997): 150-57.

Maier, Paul L. *Josephus: The Essential Writings. A New Translation*. Grand Rapids: Kregel, 1988.

Manor, Dale W. "A Brief History of Levirate Marriage as It Relates to the Bible." *Restoration Quarterly* 27.3 (1984): 129-42.

Marshall, I. Howard. "The Development of the Concept of Redemption." In *Reconciliation and Hope: New Testament Essays on Atonement and Eschatology Presented to L. L. Morris on His 60th Birthday*. Ed. Robert Banks, 153-69. Grand Rapids: Eerdmans, 1974.

Masenya, Madipoane J. "Ngwetši (Bride): The Naomi-Ruth Story from an African–South African Woman's Perspective." *Journal of Feminist Studies in Religion* 14.2 (1998): 81-90.

Matthews, Victor H. "Ruth." In *Judges and Ruth*, 207-43. New Cambridge Bible Commentary. Cambridge: Cambridge University Press, 2004.

Merrill, Eugene H. "The Book of Ruth: Narration and Shared Themes." *BSac* 142.566 (1985): 130-42.

Meyers, Carol. "Returning Home." In *A Feminist Companion to Ruth*. Ed. Athalya Brenner, 85-114. FCB 1/3. Sheffield: Sheffield Academic Press, 1993.

Miller-McLemore, Bonnie J. "Returning to the 'Mother's House': A Feminist Look at Orpah." *Christian Century* 108.13 (1991): 428-30.

Moore, Michael S. "Ruth." In J. Gordon Harris, Cheryl A. Brown, and Michael S. Moore, *Joshua, Judges, Ruth*, 293-373. New International Biblical Commentary, Old Testament Series 5. Peabody, MA: Hendrickson, 2000.

Morris, Leon. "Ruth: An Introduction and Commentary." In Arthur E. Cundall and Leon Morris, *Judges and Ruth*, 217-318. Tyndale Old Testament Commentary. Downers Grove, IL: InterVarsity Press, 1968.

Murray, John. *Redemption, Accomplished and Applied*. Repr., Edinburgh: Banner of Truth, 1961.

Neusner, Jacob. *The Mother of the Messiah in Judaism: The Book of Ruth*. Valley Forge, PA: Trinity Press International, 1993.

Nielsen, Kirsten. *Ruth*. OTL. Trans. Edward Broadbridge. Louisville: Westminster John Knox, 1997.

Ostriker, Alicia. "The Book of Ruth and the Love of the Land." *BibInt* 10.4 (2002): 343-58.

Preuss, Horst Dietrich. *Old Testament Theology.* Trans. Leo G. Perdue. OTL. 2 vols. Louisville: Westminster John Knox, 1996.

Prinsloo, Willem S. "The Theology of the Book of Ruth." *VT* 30.3 (1980): 330-41.

Rabinowitz, L., trans. "Ruth." In *Midrash Rabbah.* Ed. H. Freedman and Maurice Simon, 8:1-94. London: Soncino, 1983.

Rad, Gerhard von. *Genesis.* Trans. John H. Marks. Rev. ed. OTL. Philadelphia: Westminster, 1972.

Rashkow, Ilona. "Ruth: The Discourse of Power and the Power of Discourse." In *A Feminist Commpanion to Ruth.* Ed. Athalya Brenner, 26-41. FCB 1/3. Sheffield: Sheffield Academic Press, 1993.

Rossow, Francis C. "Literary Artistry in the Book of Ruth and Its Theological Significance." *Concordia Journal* 17.1 (1991): 12-19.

Ryan, Anne. "A Feminist Perspective on the Book of Ruth." M.A. diss. Milltown Institute, 2011.

Sakenfeld, Katherine Doob. *Ruth.* Interpretation: A Bible Commentary for Teaching and Preaching. Louisville: Westminster John Knox, 1999.

Sasson, Jack M. "The Issue of *Ge'ullāh* in Ruth." *JSOT* 5 (1978): 52-64.

————. *Ruth: A New Translation with a Philological Commentary and a Formalist-Folklorist Interpretation.* 2nd ed. Biblical Seminar 10. 1989. Repr., Sheffield: Sheffield Academic Press, 1995.

Saxegaard, Kristin M. *Character Complexity in the Book of Ruth.* Forschungen zum Alten Testament 2/47. Tübingen: Mohr Siebeck, 2010.

Schluter, Michael. "Welfare." In *Jubilee Manifesto: A Framework, Agenda and Strategy for Christian Social Reform.* Ed. Michael Schluter and John Ashcroft, 175-92. Leicester: InterVarsity Press, 2005.

Schluter, Michael, and John Ashcroft, eds. *Jubilee Manifesto: A Framework, Agenda and Strategy for Christian Social Reform.* Leicester: InterVarsity Press, 2005.

Schwartz, Regina M. *The Curse of Cain: The Violent Legacy of Monotheism.* Chicago: University of Chicago Press, 1997.

Shogren, Gary. "Redemption (NT)." *ABD* 5:654-57.

Siquans, Agnethe. "Foreignness and Poverty in the Book of Ruth: A Legal Way for a Poor Foreign Woman to Be Integrated into Israel." *JBL* 128.3 (2009): 443-52.

Stuart, Douglas. *Old Testament Exegesis: A Handbook for Students and Pastors.* 3rd ed. Louisville: Westminster John Knox Press, 2001.

Sutskover, Talia. "The Themes of Land and Fertility in the Book of Ruth." *JSOT* 34.3 (2010): 283-94.

Terrien, Samuel. *The Elusive Presence: Toward a New Biblical Theology.* New York: Harper & Row, 1978.

Thomas, Nancy J. "Weaving the Words: The Book of Ruth as Missiologically Effective Communication." *Missiology: An International Review* 30.2 (2002): 155-69.

Thompson, Thomas, and Dorothy Thompson. "Some Legal Problems in the Book of Ruth." *VT* 18.1 (1968): 79-99.

Trible, Phyllis. *God and the Rhetoric of Sexuality.* OBT. Philadelphia: Fortress, 1978.

————. *Texts of Terror: Literary-Feminist Readings of Biblical Narratives.* OBT. Philadelphia: Fortress, 1984.

Weisberg, Dvora E. "The Widow of Our Discontent: Levirate Marriage in the Bible and Ancient Israel." *JSOT* 28.4 (2004): 403-29.

Westbrook, Raymond. *Property and the Family in Biblical Law.* JSOTSup 113. Sheffield: JSOT Press, 1991.

Westermann, Claus. "Structure and Intention of the Book of Ruth." *Word and World* 19 (1999): 285-302.

Williams, Stephen N. "Providence." *NDBT* 710-15.

Wolde, Ellen van. *Ruth and Naomi.* Trans. John Bowden. London: SCM, 1997.

————. "Texts in Dialogue with Texts: Intertextuality in the Ruth and Tamar Narratives." *BibInt* 5.1 (1997): 1-28.

Wright, C. J. H. "The Ethical Authority of the Biblical Social Vision." In *Jubilee Manifesto: A Framework, Agenda and Strategy for Christian Social Reform.* Ed. Michael Schluter and John Ashcroft, 67-81. Leicester: InterVarsity Press, 2005.

————. *Living as the People of God: The Relevance of Old Testament Ethics.* Leicester: Inter-Varsity Press, 1983.

Yaron, Zvi. "Redemption: A Contemporary Jewish Understanding." *Ecumenical Review* 25 (1973): 169-79.

Ziegler, Yael. "'So Shall God Do . . .': Variations of an Oath Formula and Its Literary Meaning." *JBL* 126.1 (2007): 59-81.

Index of Authors

Index of Scripture and Other Ancient Writings